# New Methods of Teaching and Learning in Libraries

# Medical Library Association Books

The Medical Library Association (MLA) features books that showcase the expertise of health sciences librarians for other librarians and professionals.

MLA Books are excellent resources for librarians in hospitals, medical research practice, and other settings. These volumes will provide health care professionals and patients with accurate information that can improve outcomes and save lives.

Each book in the series has been overseen editorially since conception by the Medical Library Association Books Panel, composed of MLA members with expertise spanning the breadth of health sciences librarianship.

*Medical Library Association Books Panel*

Kristen L. Young, AHIP, chair
Dorothy Ogdon, AHIP, chair designate
Michel C. Atlas
Carolann Lee Curry
Kelsey Leonard, AHIP
Karen McElfresh, AHIP
JoLinda L. Thompson, AHIP
Heidi Heilemann, AHIP, board liaison

*About the Medical Library Association*

Founded in 1898, MLA is a 501(c)(3) nonprofit, educational organization of 3,500 individual and institutional members in the health sciences information field that provides lifelong educational opportunities, supports a knowledgebase of health information research, and works with a global network of partners to promote the importance of quality information for improved health to the health care community and the public.

*Books in the Series*

*The Medical Library Association Guide to Providing Consumer and Patient Health Information* edited by Michele Spatz
*Health Sciences Librarianship* edited by M. Sandra Wood
*Curriculum-Based Library Instruction: From Cultivating Faculty Relationships to Assessment* edited by Amy Blevins and Megan Inman
*Mobile Technologies for Every Library* by Ann Whitney Gleason
*Marketing for Special and Academic Libraries: A Planning and Best Practices Sourcebook* by Patricia Higginbottom and Valerie Gordon
*Translating Expertise: The Librarian's Role in Translational Research* edited by Marisa L. Conte

# New Methods of Teaching and Learning in Libraries

Ann Whitney Gleason

ROWMAN & LITTLEFIELD
Lanham • Boulder • New York • London

Published by Rowman & Littlefield
A wholly owned subsidiary of The Rowman & Littlefield Publishing Group, Inc.
4501 Forbes Boulevard, Suite 200, Lanham, Maryland 20706
www.rowman.com

Unit A, Whitacre Mews, 26-34 Stannary Street, London SE11 4AB

British Library Cataloguing in Publication Information Available

**Library of Congress Cataloging-in-Publication Data Available**

ISBN 978-1-4422-6410-6 (cloth : alk. paper)
ISBN 978-1-4422-6411-3 (pbk. : alk. paper)
ISBN 978-1-4422-6412-0 (ebook)

♾ ™ The paper used in this publication meets the minimum requirements of American
National Standard for Information Sciences Permanence of Paper for Printed Library
Materials, ANSI/NISO Z39.48-1992.

Printed in the United States of America

# Contents

# Preface

Throughout history, libraries have always been about gathering knowledge and providing education. Since the days of the great library of Alexandria, libraries have served as centers of teaching and learning. This book focuses on new methods of teaching and learning in libraries and presents possible directions for the future of teaching and learning in libraries. A solid background in teaching and learning methods and practices is given as an introduction. Emerging models of library instruction and library support of instruction will be presented with practical ways that libraries of all types can implement some of these new models. Increasingly, librarians are called upon to partner with educational faculty and community members to deliver content and support innovative educational initiatives. Since libraries reach across academic disciplines and provide resources for the greater community, they are uniquely positioned to provide services and technologies that are available to many, bringing innovation out of silos and facilitating cross-community collaborations. More and more, education is reaching beyond institutional walls and becoming a global enterprise, promising to increase educational opportunities around the world. Topics of educational innovation in libraries and the implications for planning for future services and programs will be presented.

*New Methods of Teaching and Learning in Libraries* aims to offer librarians beginning their practice of library instruction the background information and practical guidelines needed for success. Those interested in improving their instructional practice should also find topics of interest. In addition, each chapter offers new directions for delivering instruction in both physical and virtual spaces, using many different types of tools and technologies. The book is divided into three main areas of focus:

- Part I: "Teaching and Learning Practices in Library Instruction"
- Part II: "Using Educational Technology to Scaffold Learning"
- Part III: "Facilitating Learning in Library Spaces"

## PART I: TEACHING AND LEARNING PRACTICES IN LIBRARY INSTRUCTION

Background knowledge of teaching methods, educational theories, and teaching practices provides a good starting place for librarians who are called to teach in their institutions. In order to truly engage and motivate students to learn, knowledge of effective teaching methods and tools is essential. In part I, we will explore teaching methods and practices as well as guidelines for planning, delivering, and assessing educational instruction in libraries. Creative ideas, sample lesson plans, and advice from practicing librarians will be presented.

Chapter 1 focuses on the background environment of teaching and learning in libraries. It also presents an overview of learning theories and pedagogical methods. Chapter 2 focuses on teaching students skills for career success, including critical thinking, problem solving, information literacy, and evidence-based practice instruction. Active learning using group work and collaboration, problem-based learning, and other topics will be explored as ways to encourage higher-order thinking skills. Methods of planning for instruction and assessing student learning, as well as tips for improving library instruction programs, will be explored.

Chapter 3 focuses on teaching beyond the library walls, including discussions of embedded librarianship, teaching through online guides, videos, and tutorials, as well as using web conferencing and massive online open courses (MOOCs). Practical guidelines for integrating instruction with online course management systems (CMS) are presented. A well-designed CMS can be instrumental in flipping the classroom so that valuable in-class time is spent honing skills for lifelong learning. Global education initiatives and mHealth are also discussed. Open educational resources (OERs) and sharing of educational materials in learning communities will be explored.

## PART II: USING EDUCATIONAL TECHNOLOGY TO SCAFFOLD LEARNING

Educational technology can be used to support learning by serving as scaffolding for the creation of new knowledge. Libraries can also support faculty and curriculum goals directly through providing collaborative services within the library, such as writing and presentation centers, career and research services, grant-writing and grant-support services, and data management consultation. Video-conferencing facilities can be set up not only to allow institutional staff meetings but for use by faculty and students to enable collaboration with other institutions around the world or to learn and share ideas with subject experts and business people outside the institution.

Chapter 4 focuses on multimedia creation in library education, including video-creation studios, interactive displays, whiteboards, three-dimensional (3-D) printing, storytelling and digital humanities, and even virtual reality. Combining library space, technology, staff support, and librarian expertise can enable a new level of creative learning in the library. Working with faculty and the curriculum, librarians can help facilitate multimedia projects for more engaged learning, working with library resources, special collections, and archives, as well as library technology to create written or artistic works, audiovisual materials, and posters of research findings, to mention just a few ideas. Student creative work can also be displayed in the library or preserved in an online digital format for campus-wide exposure. These kinds of innovative library spaces take advanced planning and input from faculty, students, and administrators in order to be successful. Knowledge of these creative teaching and learning tools can open up a wealth of opportunities for stimulating creative learning. Chapter 5 explores the idea of ubiquitous learning through mobile technology. The future of libraries is increasingly mobile. Librarians are using tablet computers in creative ways as well as providing mobile apps, supporting mobile resources, and creating mobile websites. Library support of tablet initiatives in curriculum will also be discussed.

## PART III: FACILITATING LEARNING IN LIBRARY SPACES

Collaboration skills and successfully working in interprofessional groups, skills that are now included as objectives in many curriculum statements, can be facilitated in library spaces. The ability to communicate effectively and professionally using many types of media is also facilitated in libraries through innovative library services. The library can become an experimental space where students try out new media such as creating a video or printing in 3-D. Library spaces are also instrumental in supporting the teaching and learning missions of our institutions. As resources move from print to fully electronic, spaces previously used for book stacks are being repurposed for learning activities and study spaces. Knowledge of how spaces can be used to stimulate creativity, active learning, and collaborative group study is essential when redesigning spaces for the future.

Chapter 6 gives details about how active learning can be facilitated in collaborative library spaces. Examples of libraries that have created technology-rich spaces for collaborative learning and group work as well as facilitating individual creativity will be presented. Library spaces need to be made up of multiple areas for teaching, learning, and study. Innovative, flexible spaces that support training and presentation as well as study are explored. The lending of technology equipment in the library can support individual student work as well as faculty and curriculum goals. Staff expertise is important, and new collaborations with technology staff in libraries can help make libraries the one stop for all student needs. Chapter 7 explores creating library spaces that foster creation. These innovative rooms are often called makerspaces. Libraries are the perfect location for these creative spaces, which are used by all members of a community. Also included are innovative virtual spaces, which provide access to resources for those who might not have access to physical spaces.

Finally, chapter 8 examines the possible future of teaching and learning in libraries. What will the libraries of the future look like? Will they be completely virtual? Will they still be integral parts of communities and institutions? What might the library programs and services of the future look like? We can be assured that with well-trained teacher librarians who are familiar with the tools and technologies used for learning and who are knowledgeable about creative spaces that stimulate learning, the libraries of the future will continue to play an integral role in teaching and learning in all institutions of learning, community centers, and business centers on an increasingly global scale. Far from becoming obsolete, libraries in the future will be essential centers of teaching, learning, and the preservation of knowledge, just as they were envisioned back in the days of the great library of Alexandria.

*Part I*

# Teaching and Learning Practices in Library Instruction

*Chapter One*

# Teaching and Learning in Libraries

Teaching and learning has become an integral part of the mission of the 21st-century library. Education has always been a primary mission of libraries and is even more important in this age of information overload. Librarians are often tasked with partnering with faculty and community members to deliver content; provide spaces for teaching, learning, and study; as well as provide multimedia technologies that promote creativity and facilitate lifelong learning skills. Librarian teachers work directly with students when teaching information literacy, citation management, and other research skills. Innovative library spaces facilitate the practice of crucial job skills such as making presentations and creating multimedia communication materials, needed in the digital world we live and work in today. Librarians are partners with teachers and administrators in achieving institutional educational missions in schools, colleges, and universities. Public libraries partner with community members, local schools, and governments to provide educational services and support to community members of all ages. Although librarians in all sectors are actively engaging in teaching, very few have actual training in methods of teaching or learning theories. This chapter will provide an overview of teaching and learning in libraries and introduce the methodologies that are needed for successful teaching practices.

## A SHORT HISTORY OF EDUCATION IN LIBRARIES

One of the primary missions of libraries everywhere is education. It is obvious that schools, colleges, and universities exist to educate students, and academic libraries are a core part of their educational endeavors. Public libraries also have at their core the mission to educate their community members. The New York Public Library's mission statement includes a set of core values, and the first value is "we inspire lifelong learning by creating more able learners and researchers."[1] The mission of the Carnegie Library of Pittsburgh is "to engage our community in literacy and learning."[2] In the late 1800s and early 1900s, Andrew Carnegie built "free" libraries in many American communities in order to promote literacy and learning. His work continues today through the Carnegie Corporation, a foundation that focuses on "international peace and the advancement of education and knowledge."[3]

Throughout history, a core mission of libraries has been collecting knowledge and educating people. Libraries have existed as long as history has been written and documented. Collections of clay tablets and papyrus scrolls have been found that date back thousands of years. The earliest libraries were open only to scholars and teachers. The great library of Alexandria, the model for all libraries that came after, was theoretically a public library but in practice open only to those with the proper scholarly qualifications. In addition to private scholarly libraries, the Romans kept collections of books for reading in the public baths, which could be considered the first publicly accessible libraries.[4] During the Dark Ages, after most private and public libraries in the Western world disappeared, monastic communities began to emerge that valued literacy and they began to reestablish private libraries. At this time, learning and scholarly pursuits were limited to monastics and the nobility. During the Renaissance, the nobility began to collect classic literature and develop their own private libraries. As centers of learning emerged and universities were established, library collections again began to grow and libraries proliferated.

After the invention of the printing press, university collections surged and state and national collections began to appear. In the early American colonies, subscription libraries were created where the wealthy could pay to be members of a borrowing library. The first free public library in America, supported by taxation, opened in Peterborough, New Hampshire, in 1833. Andrew Carnegie brought libraries and learning to many more citizens by building 1,700 public libraries between 1881 and 1919.[5] Today, public libraries are the center of most communities. The American Library Association (ALA), established in 1876, promotes intellectual freedom and access to information for all. A key activity for the ALA is assisting libraries across America in "helping children and adults develop the skills they need—the ability to read and use computers—understanding that the ability to seek and effectively utilize information resources is essential in a global information society."[6]

Social developments and educational reforms were key elements in the development of modern academic libraries. Higher education was only for the elite until after the Industrial Revolution. Standardized schools and educational methods were developed with the dawn of the Industrial Revolution, but public libraries were the center of learning for the majority of people who could not afford to attend universities. Not until after World War II were more people able to attend college, and education became essential for getting ahead in life and attaining the American dream. Later, colleges established specifically for women and minorities further opened up higher education to more U.S. citizens.[7] Libraries during this time were now organized by the Dewey decimal and Library of Congress classification systems. Librarians were trained in this method of organizing materials, and there was little need for instruction to the public in the use of information resources. Not until the 1960s, with the rise of the bibliographic instruction movement, would library instruction become an important movement in U.S. colleges and universities. With the rise of the computer age and the explosion of information available on the Internet, library instruction became essential as libraries became more complex and new online catalogs and databases began to appear. Being able to teach about how to find information became an important qualification for all reference librarians. Today, library collections are measured less by how many volumes they contain and more by how connected they are to crucial resources needed by the communities they serve.[8]

## CHARACTERISTICS OF TODAY'S LEARNERS

Today's learner is quite different from the traditional student of the past. We have seen that throughout most of the history of libraries, learning was reserved for the elite. When the reforms of the 1960s opened up education to everyone, it became traditional in the United States, and in most developed countries, for those students who could afford it or who could get a scholarship to go on to college right after high school. For many years, the traditional college student was under 25 and supported by family members while attending college. Today, it is estimated that only one-third of college students fit the traditional model (see figure 1.1).[9] Statistics show that about 40 percent of college students are over 25 and more than one-third are enrolled only part time, while nearly 20 percent are working full time. Many college students today are considered nontraditional. These students are single mothers with dependent children, veterans returning to the workforce after years of military service, and young students who are earning their own way through college and do not receive any support from family members, who may be experiencing financial difficulties of their own. Problems arise when colleges and universities are still organized around providing services that work best for traditional students and do not add services for the varied needs of the new majority of nontraditional students.

## CHANGES HAPPENING IN COLLEGES AND UNIVERSITIES

In many ways, today's traditional colleges and universities have remained largely unchanged over the past several decades. Unfortunately, the changing work and economic environments are demanding that higher education institutions make sweeping changes to the way education is provided. In addition, student demographics have continued to change from the traditional residential student model to a model that incorporates lifelong learning. Because of these changes, many critical issues are facing colleges and universities today. Skill-based education for workforce development and new ways of measuring teaching and learning, both for online and traditional educational models, are needed. These issues are interrelated and should be addressed together for truly innovative and long-lasting changes to higher education not only in the United States but on a global scale in order to provide opportunities for all prospective students and to maintain the relevancy of a college education in today's world.

The United States and many other countries are going through challenging financial times, resulting in decreased state tax support for public institutions and causing tuition rates for students to increase substantially in order to compensate. Approximately 75 percent of students in the United States are enrolled in public institutions, where tuition has been more affordable for middle- to low-income students.[10] Unfortunately, the highest increases in recent years have been to public tuition rates, making a college education less affordable for the majority. Private institutions are also adjusting tuition rates

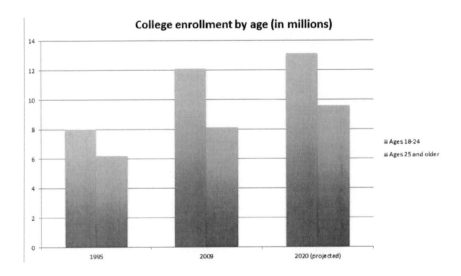

**Figure 1.1.   Projected college enrollment by age (U.S. Department of Education)**

as student enrollment drops. Student financial assistance is growing in order to meet enrollment goals, but this approach is not sustainable.[11] In countries with lingering poor economic outlooks, more people are in need of education in order to compete for shrinking jobs and to further their education so they can obtain promotional opportunities. Even though the U.S. economy is reported to be recovering, the focus of many students today is employability rather than learning for learning's sake. Higher educational institutions need to make sure they are providing the skills necessary for employment success in difficult economic times.

Related to the rising costs of education due to poor economic outlooks is the need to provide affordable, skill-based educational opportunities that directly relate to the workforce. Nearly 71 percent of U.S. college students are estimated to be nontraditional students who are 25 years of age or older, commute to campus, work at least part time while attending classes, and also have family commitments.[12] In addition, almost 90 percent of college freshmen in a 2012 research study stated that a vital reason they were attending college was to get a better job.[13] At the same time, employers are still reporting difficulty in finding college graduates who are well prepared for the jobs available with skills needed for success in the real world.[14] New models of integrating work skills into traditional college-education programs are beginning to be developed. Community colleges have traditionally been providers of workforce skill-development classes and continuing education programs and often offer flexible class times, including online learning. Public higher educational institutions are beginning to offer programs in continuing education as well, although the rising costs of all public educational programs are restrictive to some students looking to upgrade work skills. Massive open online courses, or MOOCs, seemed promising for providing educational opportunities to all, but low completion rates due to lack of relativity to actual degrees needed in order to obtain jobs has been the reality.[15]

A new model of educational innovation that has been becoming more common is online competency-based education or CBE.[16] This new model divides learning objectives into competencies or skills. Rather than the traditional model of spending a quarter or semester studying a specific subject area, students work on the individual skills needed for subject mastery on their own time at their own rate of learning. A student may spend more or less time on a skill depending on individual needs. Typically, this enables the student to complete a course of study much faster than the traditional model. CBE is also highly tailored to individual students, with ongoing assessments and online guidance and help provided from instructors only when actually needed. Programs are beginning to be offered at traditional campuses such as the University of Wisconsin's Flexible Option and Southern New Hampshire University's College for America (CfA) program.[17] Because more students can be served with these online, modularized courses, with less intervention needed from instructors, tuition costs are considerably reduced. Of course, this model is not appropriate for all students, but it may offer an alternative model for those needing flexible, affordable options.

Another pressing need for higher education is increased assessment of existing programs. With rising educational costs, the need to compete with other institutions in order to recruit the decreasing numbers of students who can afford college, and the need to stay relevant to students needing to learn work-related skills, it is imperative that institutions are able to assess their programs in order to demonstrate achievement of learning outcomes. Accreditation requirements need to be reevaluated in order to align with current needs and learning outcomes, as well as to allow for changes in educational practices. There is a great need for the development of tools and methods for accurately determining student learning and skill acquisition.[18] Assessment of quality and learning achievement in nontraditional educational models such as CBE is also lacking.

Assessment of learning in higher education typically relates directly to accreditation requirements, which are easier to track with computer-based online learning. However, higher educational institutions provide more than just subject-matter mastery. How do we measure the meaningful and often life-changing experiences that students receive from interacting with faculty, staff, and other students while attending colleges and universities? How do we measure lifelong learning skills, such as information literacy, that may be acquired outside of the classroom through interactions with library staff? How do we measure the relevancy of our programs to student career and workforce goals? These and many other questions need to be answered in order to move forward in measuring the true impact of higher education and identifying ways that educational experiences, such as library instructional programs, can be improved and be made more relevant to the goals of our current and future students.

## TEACHING AND LEARNING IN LIBRARIES

In many ways, finding, assessing, and using information, as taught by librarians, are skills crucially needed by today's nontraditional students looking for practical skills that will help them be successful at work. These skills are referred to by many different names such as "library instruction," "information literacy," or, in health-care fields, "evidence-based practice." In 2015, the Association of College and Research Libraries (ACRL) published a new "Framework for Information Literacy for Higher Education."[19] This document updates the information literacy competency standards that were published 15 years previously to reflect the rapid changes in higher education and the increasingly complex information environment. The framework cites students having a greater role in creating their own knowledge and using information and data ethically as one of the changes. Faculty members too have greater responsibilities to design educational materials that foster engagement with ideas in their disciplines. Teaching librarians also have the responsibility to identify core ideas within their area of expertise, extending learning for students, and collaborating more extensively with other faculty members.

The ACRL defines information literacy as

> the set of integrated abilities encompassing the reflective discovery of information, the understanding of how information is produced and valued, and the use of information in creating new knowledge and participating ethically in communities of learning. [20]

The ACRL sees information literacy as a "metaliteracy," meaning an overarching set of abilities that students must achieve. In this metaliteracy, students are consumers and creators of information, they participate successfully in collaboration spaces, they are engaged with information systems, and they engage in critical self-reflection in order to be self-directed in the rapidly changing information ecosystem. [21] The ACRL Framework for Information Literacy extends learning throughout the student's entire academic career, converging with all other learning goals. In order to achieve these overarching objectives, librarians must become coteachers with faculty throughout our institutions of learning.

Another important framework that is currently impacting medical education is the new Core Entrustable Professional Activities (EPAs) for entering medical residency. This framework was recently released by the Association of American Medical Colleges (AAMC) and contains a set of 13 skills that have been identified as crucial for medical students to have upon entering their residency programs. EPA number 7 addresses the important role of medical librarians teaching evidence-based practice. The description of activity 7 states that residents need to be able to identify clinical questions, build focused search questions, appraise the medical literature, and know how to access reliable and accurate medical information. [22] These are skills that many medical librarians who have been trained in evidence-based practice are well prepared to teach. Librarians can partner with medical faculty to introduce these skills throughout the curriculum during the undergraduate years of medical school in order to help students develop skills needed for a successful medical residency.

Library goals are often included in accreditation standards for educational programs such as medicine and nursing, as well as other disciplines. In partnering with faculty members to meet these accreditation goals, librarians are also increasingly becoming involved in curriculum development, helping to integrate library skills throughout the coursework.[23] Librarians are also well placed to help develop curriculum for interdisciplinary educational programs that reach across institutions, such as first-year programs and writing across the curriculum. It is important to create partnerships with faculty members to support new curriculum developments. Information literacy and evidence-based practice are skills that should not be taught in a one-shot lecture but are best integrated throughout the curriculum and aligned with student assignments in their disciplinary coursework. It's also important to include librarians on curriculum-development teams in order to integrate library skills seamlessly and to involve librarians in the curriculum as co-teachers.

In a 2005 article on developing lifelong skills in nursing education, the authors call for collaborations between faculty and librarians to develop programs that teach problem-based learning, evidence-based practice, and the efficient and effective use of nursing literature to "recognize, solve information problems and learn from information resources."[24] These are crucial skills that nurses will use throughout their career for problem solving on the job and in continuing their education. The article emphasizes that simple demonstrations of library databases given outside the curriculum are not sufficient to fully develop students' information-seeking skills. Simple database demonstrations are many times not valued by students who want and need practical skills that are immediately applicable to their coursework and research. By integrating library skills into the curriculum, weaving them throughout the course content using problem-based learning and using real-world problems, students are guided to a deeper-level learning that will translate to skills they can use after they graduate. Problem-based, information-seeking activities designed around real-world problems are much more engaging to students than one-shot lectures on the use of a database they see no pressing need to use. Integrating information skills throughout the curriculum also allows the incremental development of skills as well as practice, which ensure that the knowledge is fully integrated and transferable when applied in real-world situations.

## THE LIBRARIAN AS TEACHER

As librarians, we are often asked to assume the role of teacher in partnering with faculty in academic libraries and with community members in public libraries. With the growth of the importance of information literacy instruction and incorporating evidence-based practice in health sciences programs, as well as support for interdisciplinary programs, teaching is being recognized as a core mission of the library.[25] Unfortunately, many library school programs still do not offer much in the way of teacher training for master of information and library science (MLIS) students. Successfully collaborating with faculty to teach information literacy and critical-thinking skills requires that librarians have some background in educational theory and the psychology of learning. In academic settings, interdisciplinary programs such as first-year experience, writing across the curriculum, and other general educational requirements are providing increasing opportunities for librarians to take a lead role in teaching these important skills for student success.

Because of the trend for librarians to become more involved in the educational missions of our schools and institutions, library employers are increasingly placing a high value on educational skills when looking at job candidates. A recent study of librarian job postings found that a large percentage of postings included instructional responsibilities.[26] Another study found that instruction is now a standard responsibility required of most public-service librarians.[27] In a 2013 survey, researchers found that 87 percent of survey respondents ranked instruction as "very important" to their library.[28] Without a background in basic educational theory and psychology of learning, it is very hard for librarians to be effective teachers. In order to be truly "student centered," we should be fully versed in how students learn and be prepared to teach effectively.

In a 2012 article in the *Journal of Library Administration*, the author states that research libraries are increasingly focused on new directions, including instruction, redefinition of physical spaces, and establishment of new partnerships on and off campus.[29] This new focus brings new roles and challenges for librarians. Libraries are moving from a collection-centered model toward a new engagement-centered focus. In the article, findings are reported from a survey of the Association of Research Libraries (ARL) that studied entry-level librarian positions that had been filled within the last three years before the study. Some nontraditional qualities being sought when hiring new librarians included curiosity, adaptability, flexibility, ability to interact with users outside the library, and a passion to educate. The skills that appeared the most lacking for these positions were the interpersonal skills needed to serve as a liaison with departments or faculty. Survey respondents agreed that further training beyond library school is needed to develop the new skills needed for the changing environment of research libraries.[30]

In a study about teaching and instruction in the medical environment, 73 courses were identified from North American library and information science (LIS) programs accredited by the American Library Association (ALA), which offered at least one course with library instruction as a theme.[31] Very few institutions offered more than one course, and all offerings at all schools were elective. None of the courses identified in the study discussed library instruction in the medical environment. Considering the uniqueness of the medical library and the challenge of teaching to clinical personnel, it is extremely important for medical librarians to have continuing education opportunities available. The Medical Library Association (MLA) offers ongoing continuing education, and there are also seminars and workshops offered by medical institutions on evidence-based practice, as well as a variety of topics offered by the National Library of Medicine. Similar opportunities for other library specialties are offered through their professional organizations.

In a 2010 survey of librarians asking about their teaching practices, researchers found that most of the experienced survey respondents felt reasonably confident in their teaching skills.[32] Besides on-the-job training, over half of the respondents had undertaken continuing education courses in instruction. Teaching tasks performed ranged from informal teaching such as providing on-the-spot support (94 percent) and writing guides and training materials (93 percent) to more formal instruction such as teaching small groups (91 percent), prearranged one-to-one instruction (90 percent), and teaching large groups (79 percent). Respondents felt the most valuable knowledge learned from education courses included awareness of different learning styles and abilities, use of different techniques and methods of delivery, preparation and planning, and the need to embed instruction in the curriculum and to make delivery timely. Adopting an interactive/participative approach and the importance of feedback, evaluation, and reflection were also listed as important.[33]

So how can new librarians learn these important skills needed for the teaching role if they are not offered in standard MLIS programs? Some librarians are able to take advanced coursework in education, instructional technology, or instructional design. These candidates are in high demand. But not everyone has the time or funds to complete another degree. Many librarians must learn on the job from other, more experienced librarians who may also not have sufficient educational backgrounds. As mentioned previously, continuing education is crucial, especially for special libraries. If the MLIS program does not offer educational courses, taking one or two courses in education while in library school could help prepare students for the job market and eventual job duties, especially if they are interested in teaching. Working as a graduate assistant can also be good training, especially if done along with taking coursework in education. Considering the increased emphasis on teaching in libraries, at least a basic background in education will better prepare library school students for successfully answering questions during job interviews and help them develop teaching skills and educational practices. Continuing education courses and MOOCs are another way to learn more about educational theories and practices to enhance library job skills.[34] In the next section, we will cover a basic overview of learning and instructional theories. This section is not meant to fully cover the complex field of educational theory but will lay a foundation for its discussion in the rest of the chapters of this book.

# IMPORTANT INSTRUCTIONAL THEORIES

Key terms:

- Active learning
- Bloom's taxonomy
- Constructivist learning model
- Flipped classroom
- Kolb's experiential learning cycle
- Problem-based learning and case-based learning
- Scaffolding
- Social learning

When we refer to student's having responsibility for creating their own knowledge, we are using the constructivist learning model. New ideas in teaching and learning typically follow this constructivist model, and it works well for guiding library instruction. This model of learning proposes that students construct knowledge by combining previous knowledge with new information. Education has been criticized in the past for having no connection with real life.[35] In the modern world of complex knowledge, big data, and information overload, there is a pressing need for people to learn how to efficiently find and assess information. Problem-solving and critical-thinking skills are needed for success at most jobs, as well as creative thinking to find solutions and inventions to solve the problems of modern life. The focus should be not on the results of teaching as measured by standardized testing but on the learning process so that the goal will be to motivate the learner in his or her own learning process. A teacher's main role is then to help learners recall and activate their prior knowledge in order to build new knowledge.

Constructivist learning theories come from educational theorists such as John Dewey, Jean Piaget, Jerome Bruner, Lev Vygotsky, David Kolb, and Maria Montessori.[36] *Active learning* and *discovery learning* are other terms for the same type of learning, where learners actively construct their own knowledge through exploration. Instead of lectures or presentations, students engage in activities in the classroom. This is also referred to as the *flipped classroom.* Some important concepts in constructivist learning include:

- Students must actively construct their own meaning in order to process and transfer knowledge.
- Students build new learning by making connections between prior knowledge and new information.
- Student learning is enhanced in social settings when ideas are compared and shared with others.
- Students learn best through real-world or "authentic" tasks.

The teacher's job in this environment is to facilitate learning. The teacher asks questions or guides the students to ask questions. The teacher also provides scaffolding for learning, which is defined as a practice or technology that supports the creation of new knowledge in complex learning environments. Scaffolding provides a supportive framework that guides student learning through the steps needed for discovery. It is also very important for teachers to provide time for student reflection on teacher feedback and on their own learning process.

The learning environment is key when practicing constructivist learning. Learning is an active process where the attention is put on acquiring higher-order thinking and problem-solving skills, not memorization of facts.[37] Often this kind of learning also has social and collaborative aspects when students are working together on projects involving real-world tasks. The learning environment frequently involves technology and group collaboration spaces to facilitate active learning. Students are encouraged to explore relationships between facts and to construct mental frameworks for new information. With the available technology, students act as designers using multimedia tools to analyze, access, and interpret information, as well as to organize knowledge and communicate it to others.

The goal of the constructivist teacher is to create an environment where learners are active in the process of creating new knowledge. Teachers are responsible for creating support mechanisms for learning. Technology such as a course management system can also be used to scaffold the process of active learning by providing tools and resources for guiding learning. Library resources such as LibGuides can also serve as scaffolding for learning. Active learning methods require that the instructor become less of a lecturer and more of a "guide on the side" or facilitator of learning. Students are encouraged to use critical thinking and reflect on their learning process.[38] The instructor is then able to move around the classroom, assisting students as they work on activities related to their research or problem solving a "real-world" case presented by the instructor or librarian. Active learning is more engaging for students because it allows them to express ideas and pose their own questions. Since students are required to participate in this mode of instruction, their focus on the content is much greater than if they were attending a passive lecture. Librarians can benefit from using this method by decreasing repetitive lectures and spending more time facilitating the learning process by posing questions or problems and helping students individually as they work on their own or in groups.

In a guest column in *Reference and User Services Quarterly*, the author discusses the important role of information literacy in helping students to become motivated, lifelong learners.[39] Skills in critical thinking, problem solving, communication, and creativity are increasingly important outcomes to education in the 21st century.[40] Students typically go through several stages of intellectual development, from knowledge as facts to having opinions about what they are learning to evaluating and reasoning using good logic and evidence to finally establishing a commitment to lifelong learning and intellectual development. Most college-age students are in the first stages of intellectual development according to a classic study on college student cognitive development.[41] Information literacy instruction can help students move to higher-order thinking and so can be crucial to college students' success in their academic careers.

The stages of intellectual development have been well defined through Bloom's taxonomy, which has been used for many years by teachers to design educational programs (see figure 1.2).[42] Benjamin Bloom divided learning into three domains: cognitive, affective, and psychomotor. In adult education, we are mostly concerned with the cognitive domain. Bloom identified six types of learning activities in the cognitive domain: remembering, comprehension, application, analysis, synthesis, and evaluation. The higher-order learning activities such as analysis, synthesis, and evaluation are related to higher-order cognitive skills.[43] These theories of intellectual development are important guideposts that can be used to identify where students are in their development and to help them grow intellectually by facilitating higher-order thinking skills through activities where students are encouraged to analyze, synthesize, and evaluate information. Information literacy goals often involve developing these important kinds of thinking skills that will be important for students' personal growth and professional development for the rest of their lives.

In a keynote address at a workshop on lifelong learning, the speaker proposed that information literacy can be thought of as the foundation of learning in our increasingly complex information and technological society.[44] Information literacy instruction teaches information practices that will help students be effective professionally, civically, and in their personal lives.[45] Information literacy can be the transformative key to changing a society characterized by information overload into a learning society. It can be transformational because it encourages deeper learning and empowers learners to seek and access the information they need in order to take their place in this modern, complex learning society.

The "learning pyramid" is a useful visualization showing why the active learning methods emphasized in the constructivist model are so important. The learning pyramid idea seems to have been started in the 1960s by National Training Laboratories (NTL).[46] Although not backed up by actual statistical studies, the idea is that only 10 percent of what people read is retained; 20 percent of what they hear, as in a lecture, is retained; and 30 percent of what is seen in a visual way is retained. Combining methods of learning, 50 percent of what is both seen and heard, as in a live demonstration, video, or field trip, is retained. Continuing toward the base of the pyra-

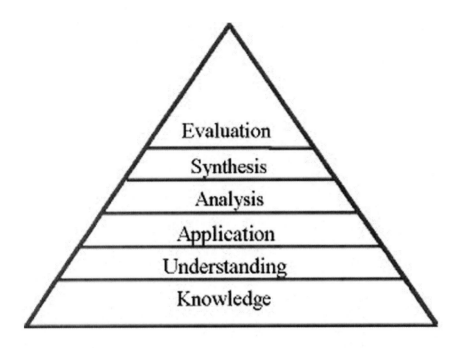

**Figure 1.2.   Bloom's taxonomy, cognitive domain**

mid, 70 percent of what a learner says or writes is retained, which indicates that having students write papers or do presentations is very effective. At the base of the pyramid, at 90 percent retention, is having learners speak while they do an activity, which indicates that group activities simulating real-world experiences are the best way to learn and retain learning. Keep in mind that different people learn in different ways, and some material may be best learned in a less interactive way depending on the situation. No one model can explain the complexities of human learning, but it makes sense that teaching methods that approach real life and engage students will be the most effective.

Problem-based learning (PBL) and case-based learning (CBL) are types of learning that follow from the constructivist model. The constructivist model of learning stresses that learning is best facilitated when learners interact with their environment to construct knowledge, usually in a social setting. Especially useful in medical education as well as other practical disciplines such as business, PBL uses real-life cases or problems to facilitate student learning through problem-solving exercises. CBL grew out of PBL and is more of a guided approach where the expertise of the instructor is important in steering the discussion and providing an accurate context for learning. In PBL, the instructor's role is more passive. While both approaches involve group work, PBL encourages self-directed learning as well as group discussion.[47] Students need to be independent information seekers who know where and how to search for information. They need to be able to assess the quality of the information they find in order to solve real-world problems. Librarians are instrumental in teaching this process and can be partners with disciplinary faculty experts to guide students through the process with the goal of creating independent learners. Learning in groups is also a hallmark of PBL. In many health sciences programs, curriculum reform is beginning to formally integrate PBL or CBL and other group learning methods into the curriculum after recognizing the importance of the skills learned through these activities. Group learning can also be a motivation factor for increased student learning.

Learning is enhanced in a social setting according to Lev Vygotsky, a teacher and psychologist who wrote in the 1960s and 1970s about social learning. Vygotsky felt that learning is always occurring and therefore cannot be separated from the social context.[48] Instructional methods that support social learning include group projects, interdisciplinary collaborations, debates among students or student groups, and students working together to achieve a challenging task. Collaborative communities of learners work together on research projects and share the results by producing a final performance or report. Each student in a group brings their own previous knowledge and expertise to the group, magnifying the learning experience for all group members. An example of CBL in library instruction that can be a very successful model involves a faculty member serving as subject expert and a librarian providing instruction in database searching working together to find an answer to a real-world case. Students search for information and discuss their results, learning both how to effectively search for information and subject expertise.

Learning is an individual process, and each learner has his or her own way of processing information. In the 1970s, David Kolb published his Experiential Learning Cycle to illustrate four stages that learners go through when presented with a new learning experience.[49] Learners are typically more comfortable in one stage over the others, but they need to progress through all stages in order for effective learning to occur. The stages are a cycle, so you can enter at any point, and all stages are mutually supportive. The stages are concrete experience, reflective observation, abstract conceptualization, and active experimentation. The importance of this theory to teaching is that learning activities should involve multiple ways of experiencing, experimenting, conceptualizing, and reflecting in order to be effective for all types of learners.

Learning can be informal, such as learning a new skill or exploring personal interests. This kind of learning is very self-directed. Public libraries are instrumental in this kind of learning. Professional learning, which takes place in order to do work or improve work-related skills, can also be self-directed. Hospital libraries, law libraries, and other work-related information centers support this kind of learning. Formal learning, which is done in schools, colleges, and universities, relies on specialized subject-matter collections and access to a wide variety of resources and data repositories that must be timely, accurate, and broad in scope.[50]

## THE LIBRARIAN'S ROLE IN TEACHING AND LEARNING

Library liaison roles have changed dramatically, especially in higher education, as new models of learning have transformed teaching.[51] New technologies, the growth of big data, new research methods, and the changes in scholarly publishing and dissemination of research have changed the focus of library liaisons from merely preserving and sharing information to direct support and participation in the processes of instruction, research, and scholarship. A new model of "engaged" librarianship is emerging, which "seeks to enhance scholar productivity, to empower learners, and to participate in the entire lifecycle of the research, teaching, and learning process."[52] This new model is outwardly focused and requires strong relationships with the faculty and administrators of our institutions and research centers. The engaged librarian partners with faculty and researchers in order to help them share and disseminate research and data, integrate knowledge resources into the curriculum, and teach the lifelong skills needed for problem solving and information finding. Engaged librarians are also helping researchers better manage their data and disseminate it to the widest possible audience.

These new roles make it necessary for librarians to develop new skills in teaching and learning—not only in working with students but in working with faculty and researchers of an institution as well as community members. Traditional one-shot guest lectures within subject areas can be an important component of library work but not on the scale needed to address broad curriculum goals and institution-wide instructional mandates. Library instruction can be much more successful when integrated into courses at key times as students are developing research skills throughout their course of study. Online tutorials and instructional materials can provide scaffolding for learning information-finding skills, extending the reach of librarians to many more students than traditional methods. This integrated model takes advance planning and collaboration with faculty and administrators. Thus, librarians should be included in the process of curriculum reform and the development of new programs.

We will use the ideas introduced in this chapter in exploring the actual practice of education in much more detail in the following chapters of this book. The next chapter will give an overview of the practices of teaching and learning in libraries and the evolving academic environment, which drives the adoption of new methods of teaching. Practical guidelines for improving teaching and instructional programs in libraries will be presented. The importance of library instruction to student academic success as well as lifelong learning also will be discussed.

## NOTES

1. New York Public Library, "NYPL's Mission Statement," NYPL.org, accessed June 30, 2015, www.nypl.org/help/about-nypl/mission.

2. Carnegie Library of Pittsburgh, "Mission and Vision," CLPGH.org, accessed June 30, 2015, http://clpgh.org/about/mission.html.

3. Carnegie Corporation of New York, "Mission and Vision," Carnegie.org, accessed June 30, 2015, http://carnegie.org/about-us/mission -and-vision/.

4. Barbara Krasner-Khait, "Survivor: The History of the Library," *History Magazine*, October/November 2001, accessed June 30, 2015, www.history-magazine.com/libraries.html.

5. Ibid.

6. American Library Association, "About ALA," ALA.org, accessed June 30, 2015, www.ala.org/aboutala/about-ala.

7. Donna L. Gilton, "Information Literacy Instruction: A History in Context," University of Rhode Island website, accessed June 30, 2015, www.uri.edu/artsci/lsc/Faculty/gilton/InformationLiteracyInstruction.

8. Ibid.

9. Jenna Johnson, "Today's Typical College Students Often Juggle Work, Children and Bills with Coursework," *Washington Post*, September 14, 2013, accessed June 30, 2015, www.washingtonpost.com/local/education/todays-typical-college-students-often-juggle-work-children-and-bills-with-coursework/2013/09/14/4158c8c0–1718–11e3–804b-d3a1a3a18f2c_story.html.

10. John Ebersole, "Top Issues Facing Higher Education in 2014," *Forbes*, January 13, 2014, accessed June 30, 2015, www.forbes.com/sites/johnebersole/2014/01/13/top-issues-facing-higher-education-in-2014/.

11. Jonathan M. Brand, "Resolving Higher Education's Challenges," *Huffington Post*, February 26, 2014, accessed June 30, 2015, www.huffingtonpost.com/jonathan-m-brand/resolving-higher-educations-challenges_b_4861024.html.

12. Michelle R. Weise, "Got Skills? Why Online Competency-Based Education Is the Disruptive Innovation for Higher Education," *Educause Review*, November 10, 2014, accessed June 30, 2015, www.educause.edu/ero/article/got-skills-why-online-competency-based-education-disruptive-innovation-higher-education.

13. Ibid.

14. Brand, "Resolving Higher Education's Challenges."

15. Kevin Carey, "Here's What Will Truly Change Higher Education: Online Degrees That Are Seen as Official," *New York Times*, accessed June 30, 2015, www.nytimes.com/2015/03/08/upshot/true-reform-in-higher-education-when-online-degrees-are-seen-as-official.html?_r=0&abt=0002&abg=1.

16. Weise, "Got Skills?"

17. Ibid.

18. Ebersole, "Top Issues Facing Higher Education."

19. Association of College and Research Libraries, "Framework for Information Literacy for Higher Education," ALA.org, accessed June 30, 2015, www.ala.org/acrl/standards/ilframework.

20. Ibid.

21. Ibid.

22. Association of American Medical Colleges, "Core Entrustable Professional Activities for Entering Residency," AAMC.org, accessed June 30, 2015, https://members.aamc.org/eweb/DynamicPage.aspx?Action=Add&ObjectKeyFrom=1A83491A-9853-4C87-86A4-F7D95601C2E2&WebCode=PubDetailAdd&DoNotSave=yes&ParentObject=CentralizedOrderEntry&ParentDataObject=Invoice%20Detail&ivd_formkey=69202792-63d7-4ba2-bf4e-a0da41270555&ivd_prc_prd_key=E3229B10-BFE7-4B35-89E7-512BBB01AE3B.

23. Joan Lippincott, Anu Vedantham, and Kim Duckett, "Libraries as Enablers of Pedagogical and Curricular Change," *Educause Review*, accessed June 30, 2015, www.educause.edu/ero/article/libraries-enablers-pedagogical-and-curricular-change.

24. Alan G. Barnard, Robyn E. Nash, and Michael O'Brien, "Information Literacy: Developing Lifelong Skills through Nursing Education," *Journal of Nursing Education* 44, no. 11 (2005): 505–10.

25. Dani Brecher and Kevin Michael Klipfel, "Education Training for Instruction Librarians: A Shared Perspective," *Communications in Information Literacy* 8, no. 1 (2014): 43–49.

26. Russell A. Hall, "Beyond the Job Ad: Employers and Library Instruction," *College and Research Libraries* 74, no. 1 (2013): 24–38.

27. Kimberly Davies-Hoffman, Barbara Alvarez, Michelle Costello, and Debby Emerson, "Keeping Pace with Information Literacy Instruction for the Real World: When Will MLS Programs Wake Up and Smell the LILACs?" *Communications in Information Literacy* 7, no. 1 (2013): 9–23.

28. Hall, "Beyond the Job Ad."

29. James L. Mullins, "Are MLS Graduates Being Prepared for the Changing and Emerging Roles That Librarians Must Now Assume within Research Libraries?" *Journal of Library Administration* 52, no. 1 (2012): 124–32.

30. Ibid.

31. Ellen Gay Detlefsen, "Teaching about Teaching and Instruction on Instruction: A Challenge for Health Sciences Library Education," *Journal of the Medical Library Association: JMLA* 100, no. 4 (2012): 244.

32. Laura Bewick and Sheila Corrall, "Developing Librarians as Teachers: A Study of Their Pedagogical Knowledge," *Journal of Librarianship and Information Science* 42, no. 2 (2010): 97–110.

33. Ibid.

34. Hall, "Beyond the Job Ad."

35. Eeva-Liisa Eskola, "University Students' Information Seeking Behaviour in a Changing Learning Environment: How Are Students' Information Needs, Seeking and Use Affected by New Teaching Methods?" *Information Research* 4, no. 2 (1998): 4–2.

36. Susan E. Cooperstein and Elizabeth Kocevar-Weidinger, "Beyond Active Learning: A Constructivist Approach to Learning," *Reference Services Review* 32, no. 2 (2004): 141–48.

37. Beth S. Woodard, "Technology and the Constructivist Learning Environment: Implications for Teaching Information Literacy Skills," *Research Strategies* 19, no. 3 (2003): 181–92.

38. Lisa Shamchuk and Leah Plouffe, "MacEwan University Library's Pedagogical Shift Using Active Learning Activities during First-Year Information Literacy Sessions," *College and Research Libraries News* 74, no. 9 (2013): 480–95.

39. Gabrielle K. W. Wong, "Facilitating Students' Intellectual Growth in Information Literacy Teaching," *Reference and User Services Quarterly* (2010): 114–18.

40. Ibid.

41. Joanne Kurfiss, "Sequentiality and Structure in a Cognitive Model of College Student Development," *Developmental Psychology* 13, no. 6 (1977): 565.

42. Old Dominion University, "Bloom's Taxonomy." Old Dominion University website, accessed June 30, 2015, https://www.maine.gov/doe/arts/resources/bloom.html.

43. Wong, "Facilitating Students' Intellectual Growth."

44. Christine S. Bruce, *Information Literacy as a Catalyst for Educational Change: A Background Paper* (Rockhampton, QLD: Central Queensland University Press, 2004): 8–19.

45. Ibid.

46. Char Booth, *Reflective Teaching, Effective Learning: Instructional Literacy for Library Educators* (Chicago: American Library Association, 2011).

47. H. S. Barrow, "Problem-Based Learning in Medicine and Beyond," *Bringing Problem-Based Learning to Higher Education: Theory and Practice* (1996): 3–12.

48. Learning Theories, "Lev Vygotsky and Social Learning Theories," Northern Arizona University website, accessed June 30, 2015, http://jan.ucc.nau.edu/lsn/educator/edtech/learningtheorieswebsite/vygotsky.

49. Saul McLeod, "Kolb—Learning Styles," SimplyPsychology.org, accessed June 30, 2015, http://www.simplypsychology.org/learning-kolb.html.

50. Gary Marchionini and Hermann Maurer, "The Roles of Digital Libraries in Teaching and Learning," *Communications of the ACM* 38, no. 4 (1995): 67–75.

51. Janice Jaguszewski and Karen Williams, *New Roles for New Times: Transforming Liaison Roles in Research Libraries* (Washington, DC: Association of Research Libraries, 2013).

52. Ibid.

*Chapter Two*

# Teaching Students Skills for Career and Life Success

Before exploring innovative new approaches to teaching and learning, it is important to step back and examine the current state of library instruction, exploring why we teach, what we teach, and how we teach. Librarians know that the skills we teach for effective researching and information literacy are essential for lifelong learning and success in both academic work and professional work. Unfortunately, librarians are not necessarily recognized as partners in teaching and learning by the institutions and communities we serve. In a 2011 study of college students' information-seeking behaviors, researchers found that students rarely sought out librarian help on research assignments.[1] The researchers used anthropological methods to observe student behavior when conducting research. Anthropological methods are a relatively new and enlightening way of assessing library programs. Students are observed as they interact with resources and spaces in the library. The researchers found that although today's students have been raised as "digital natives," very few study participants actually knew how to conduct good research. The students in the study tended to overuse Google and preferred simple searches, even when using library databases. They lacked an understanding of search logic and were not able to evaluate Internet sources reliably. Even when using Google, students were not knowledgeable about how the information is organized and displayed, so they tended to choose research topics depending on how much information they could find easily with a simple search. Even those few students who were aware of library databases tended to enter Google-like searches, rendering either too few or too many results. Most students observed in the study were unaware of how to narrow their search results. Despite the fact that many realized their limitations in doing research, not one student in the study asked a librarian for help.

In the 2011 study, it was found that students who had attended library instruction sessions or even short orientation sessions showed greater research proficiency than those who had not attended any sessions.[2] This underlines the need for library instruction to be integrated into all students' learning experiences at some point in their academic career. Students are often unaware of their lack of information literacy, and many overestimate their knowledge and ability to do quality research. The study authors found that most students, as well as faculty members, were unaware that librarians do work related to helping students do research. Many were unsure what librarians do besides giving directions to the book stacks. Faculty members have the most interactions with students and are the key to informing students about library resources and how librarians can help. Unfortunately, many faculty members in the study also had low expectations for librarians. A study by the ITHAKA Group shows that library directors view the library as serving a teaching role, but faculty members see the library as merely a purchaser of resources.[3] Many faculty members also incorrectly assume students learned research skills from other classes and overestimate their students' abilities. There is a crucial need to improve, increase, and market library instruction programs to address these needs.

## INCREASED NEED FOR LIBRARY INSTRUCTION

In a study of the amount of time librarians spent in the teaching role at Washington State University, the University of Maryland, and the University of Kansas, it was found that teaching time had significantly increased in the ten years reviewed (see figure 2.1).[4] This study reflects a huge growth in the amount of professional time librarians spend in teaching activities. The *Chronicle of Higher Education* reports that a survey of American library directors in all four-year colleges and universities showed that of the 33 percent who responded to the survey, 97 percent of the library directors felt that one of the most important priorities was teaching information literacy to undergraduates.[5] This points out a growing need to hire librarians who have teaching skills. There was a noticeable decline in library directors who felt that supporting faculty research was a top priority, from 85 percent in 2010 to about 70 percent in 2013. This shows a major shift in priorities away from research and library collections toward direct instruction of students by librarians.

In a recent survey of medical library instruction, the study authors found that the librarians surveyed struggled to provide meaningful instructional programs due to a lack of faculty and student participation as well as staffing limitations.[6] Over 96 percent of respondents reported they offer some level of training programs. Database searching was the top type of instruction

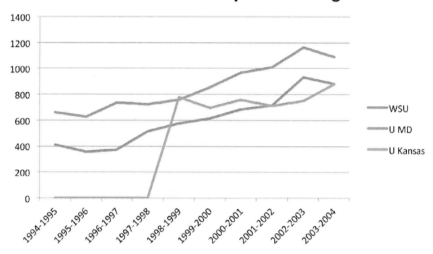

**Figure 2.1. Information literacy classes taught (Walter, 2008)**

offered by over 97 percent of the librarians surveyed, followed by library orientations offered by over 81 percent. Bibliographic management and information literacy instruction was offered by almost half the respondents. Very few offered other types of instruction such as evidence-based medicine, technology training, or research methods. More than half of the respondents are moving from prescheduled workshops to offering instruction as needed, when clients request it, due to declining enrollments. Most librarians offered individual or small-group instruction or classroom lectures. Only around 20 percent offered video or online tutorials of any kind. Very few offered webinar-type instruction.

Lack of participation in prescheduled instruction sessions was the number one challenge faced in library instruction programs.[7] Reasons reported included lack of time for students or researchers to attend, lack of appeal of the sessions offered, poor marketing strategies, and lack of time for librarians to develop appealing educational programs. Having a strong presence in the academic institution at meetings and events as well as building rapport with students and faculty are key marketing strategies but take time and adequate staffing. Reduced staffing is also a big issue since good instruction takes time for planning, delivering, and assessing instruction. Other issues reported are a lack of proper training to provide needed distance-education sessions, problems with technology tools, the need to collaborate with faculty to do instruction integrated with course research projects, and the large variety of user needs to be served in the complex academic institution of the 21st century.[8] It's also very important to get user feedback in order to keep instruction current and appealing to users, which takes even more time for library staff to conduct assessment activities. Limited staffing also impacts the ability to keep self-help websites, guides, and tutorials current and engaging. Clearly, staff who are willing and able to provide quality instruction programs in libraries are badly needed.

At Stony Brook University, librarians found that in-library workshops held at the Health Sciences Library often were not well attended. Moving instruction to a location more convenient for the clients greatly improved attendance. For example, when teaching evidence-based medicine to residents, librarians had much greater attendance when presenting during the resident noon conferences. These sessions are well attended because residents are used to being present at this time for other activities such as chart reviews. The department also provides lunch for some of these sessions, which is a further incentive for attendance. Some departments require attendance and have a sign-in sheet. Most workshops scheduled in the library are poorly attended, with the exception of training for first-year medical students. At this level of medical training, the students are used to large-group classroom instruction, and the sessions are well attended in the computer lab when required by instructors.

Best practice for library instruction is to offer customized services for the specific needs and for the specific intended audience. This may be a rather large challenge with limited staffing. Also key to successful instruction is customizing the training materials and teaching methods to be useful and engaging to the specific audience. Once that happens, word spreads to other departments that the library offers useful and engaging sessions, customized to their schedules, and convenient to their locations. Staff training is very important in offering interactive sessions using real-world problems that the audience can relate to, as well as using active learning methods, which engage the audience. Each library setting will be different, so it's important to put users first and tailor instruction programs to meet unique needs. Assessment is also important in creating an environment of continuous improvement. This is a tall order for libraries but one that is sorely needed in order to keep our programs current and relevant.

## Importance of Library Instruction

The instruction that libraries provide cuts across curriculum lines. The skills we teach can increase student success in all courses across the student's academic career and beyond. The skills learned from information literacy can provide crucial skills for successful careers as well as enhance people's personal lives, where information finding can be just as, or even more, crucial.

Whether you call it information literacy, research skills, evidence-based practice, or lifelong learning, it's the ability to sift through the massive amount of information available and choose, evaluate, and use meaningful, quality information. If done right, library instruction can also develop critical-thinking skills, problem-solving skills, and other communication and technology skills crucial to career success.

At James Madison University (JMU), a librarian serving the College of Business contacted members of the local business community in order to assess the importance of information literacy instruction in business careers.[9] While it is generally understood that being able to find and use information to inform business practices and decisions is important for business leaders, business faculty are not typically known for their collaboration with librarians. In the JMU study, business community members were asked what types of information they used in their work, what information tools they used, what activities they did that were informed by research, and what skills they felt were necessary for new graduates. While interviewees articulated that "soft skills" such as communication, problem solving, and technology were important for business graduates to have, they did not equate information literacy as taught by librarians to be related to those skills. While they agreed that new graduates needed to be able to think critically, synthesize information, and present research findings, they felt that generic information sources such as Google were generally sufficient to find the information needed.[10] While interviewees did not recognize the skills needed as information literacy skills, it is still apparent that today's graduate needs these skills, no matter what name you give them. The focus needs to be on the skills and not the term *information literacy*, which is typically only used by librarians. Broadening the definition of library instruction to include research and technology skills could be one way to show how library instruction aligns with the skills needed for business success.

## NEW CAREER PATHS FOR LIBRARIANS

New positions in libraries related to instruction and instructional design are becoming prevalent in library job listings. A search of job postings on the American Library Association (ALA) JobLIST website during the summer of 2015 revealed that over 117 of the approximately 350 listings either had "instruction" in the title or in the job description. Eighty-six more listings had "teaching" in the title or description. Some of the most common job titles listed included instruction and reference librarian, teaching and learning librarian, outreach and instruction librarian, instruction and online learning librarian, and information literacy librarian. Scholarly communications librarian and assessment librarian also included instructional components in the job listing.[11] In a 2006 article analyzing librarian job advertisements, the author found that library instruction was becoming increasingly important in all types of librarian positions.[12] This emphasis on instruction is creating a work environment that values librarians with instruction skills and encourages enhancement of those skills. Instructional design librarians are engaged in developing instructional products for libraries, so they also need to analyze how people learn, identify the contexts in which people will learn best, create instructional strategies that will promote learning for specific audiences, and create learning objectives for library instruction. Most of the job advertisements reviewed asked for an MLIS (master of library and information science) degree, but some listed an equivalent degree, such as a master's in education or instructional technology. Besides instructional skills, most jobs also required web authoring and publishing skills and proficiency with multimedia software. Familiarity with emerging instructional technologies was also preferred.

Instructional design librarians are engaged in creating online tutorials, guides, and learning modules. They must keep current with emerging instructional technologies, and they take the lead in creating and assessing library instruction programs. Some positions engage instructional design librarians in creating online resources for academic departmental curricula beyond library instruction.[13] Key skills needed include the ability to create and assess online instructional modules, the ability to conduct instructional programs, and proficiency with existing and emerging instructional technologies. Surprisingly, only 40 percent of job advertisements specified that the candidate should have knowledge of instructional methods and learning theories.[14] Only one-third of the jobs required a background in instructional design even when "instructional design" appeared in the job title. This reflects a disconnect between library degree programs, which often lack courses in instructional methods, and the need for librarians trained in instructional methods. This disconnect is especially of concern with the documented growth of instruction in libraries and the increased demand for instructional designers in library settings.

## EDUCATIONAL METHODS FOR LIBRARY INSTRUCTION

Since library science programs often do not adequately train librarians for the level of instruction needed in today's libraries, new librarians or those interested in doing more teaching need to find ways to gain the needed skills in order to be successful. While training can be obtained through professional development and continuing education courses, the fact remains that many new librarians are thrown into instruction with little or no training. Finding a seasoned librarian to serve as a mentor can be of great help, but many seasoned librarians also have not had adequate training in teaching practices. It takes time and effort to build a good teaching practice, and sometimes you learn more from the failures than you do from the successes. Constant reflection on your instructional practices and working to find ways to improve will result in continuing growth. The following is an overview of some of the most prevalent educational methods, which can help you reflect upon your current instructional practice. It is worth noting that not all practices and methods work with all students or in all situations. It is crucial to know your specific audience and institutional culture well so that you can match educational methods to specific needs. Also, individuals will have different strengths and abilities, and some methods will work better for individual teachers than others. Part of improving instructional practice involves getting to know your own teaching style, emphasizing your strengths, and working to improve any weaknesses.

## ESSENTIAL TEACHING SKILLS

In a book released by Independent School Management (ISM), 20 principles for teaching excellence are proposed with scales for self-assessment.[15] These principles are similar to the principles needed for good leadership. Teachers can be thought of as leaders of students and need to be managers of their classrooms on a daily basis. The principles include being authoritative and current in an academic field, holding high expectations and standards of students but allowing for individual needs, having clear goals and objectives that are integrated into the teaching process, and ensuring that active learning takes up half of the class time.[16] Other principles that are important for teaching at any level include giving students responsibility for their own learning, showing a professional interest in students, individualizing instruction, reinforcing good performance in a timely manner, and recognizing excellence and effort by giving positive feedback.

Active learning is a key concept for stimulating higher-order thinking skills. Active learning in the classroom is critical because it involves students in actively creating their own knowledge, as taught in the constructivist model. There are many activities teachers can use in class sessions to encourage active learning. The two most important concepts that should be reflected in an interactive session are that (1) students are doing something besides passively listening to a lecture and (2) students are encouraged to reflect on a problem, issue, or concept. On a basic level, adding small-group discussion, in-class quizzes, or question-answer sessions will introduce active learning. To reach the higher levels of learning represented by Bloom's taxonomy, problem solving and group work should also be introduced into activities. The social aspect of encouraging students to work together stimulates higher-order learning since students can practice skills and learn from each other. [17] Some activities that foster active learning include case-based learning or problem solving, debate or group discussion, using clickers or online polling to answer questions, and collaborative concept mapping. Examples of specific activities for encouraging higher-order thinking skills include "think, pair, share" and "thinking-aloud pair problem-solving." The think, pair, share activity involves the instructor posing a higher-order question and then giving students time to think about the answer. Next, they discuss ideas with a partner. A follow-up discussion with the entire class usually follows. In thinking-aloud pair problem-solving, a case study is posed and students work with a partner to solve the problem. One is the explainer and the other the questioner for a period of time, and then they switch roles. [18] These types of activities are easy to incorporate into a variety of library instruction sessions.

Beyond excellence in subject matter and active learning teaching practices, it is hard to quantify the qualities that make up a great teacher. Student feedback on course evaluations and services such as ratemyprofessors.com only tell part of the story. In an ongoing study of college professors identified as excellent teachers by their former students, researchers have tried to quantify some of the qualities that make someone a great teacher. One of the main findings of the study has been that excellent teachers foster an environment of deep learning and motivate students to create their own knowledge. [19] They accomplish these goals by having students answer questions or solve problems that the students care about. They allow students to explore ideas and receive feedback before being formally graded. They challenge students to question their existing beliefs, helping the students to create new paradigms. [20] Excellent teachers also foster a class environment where it is safe to question and explore, where the teacher is not always the "expert," and where students feel challenged to delve deeply into questions and problems that make a difference. Also, effective teachers are clear about course objectives, they are perceived as fair in grading practices, and they are organized so that students know what to expect as well as what is expected of them in the learning process.

## THE IMPORTANCE OF LESSON PLANNING

Studies have shown that student achievement is significantly higher when teachers use structured methods of planning. [21] Structured lesson planning also improves the chances that a session will be successful and lesson outcomes will be achieved. Planning for instruction gives teachers a chance to visualize the class session and specifically plan for how learning goals will be achieved, as well as giving the teacher a chance to reflect on the objectives for the class session. Experienced teachers are less dependent on lesson planning since they may have presented the material many times in the past, but novice teachers or those preparing to teach new material could benefit from using a lesson planning model. Studies have also shown that planning for teaching is mainly a cognitive process. Much of the planning time consists of thinking about the lesson rather than actually writing the plan; therefore, planning can be described as a mental process. [22]

There are many models taught to student teachers for planning lessons. Some K–12 school districts require lesson plans to be formatted in a specific, district-approved way. Lesson plans are usually optional in a higher education setting but may be required for new teachers by their supervisor. One of the most commonly used models for planning the steps in a lesson is the Madeline Hunter Instructional Theory into Practice, or ITIP, model. This model has been in use since 1984 and consists of seven components that should be considered when planning lessons. These components are not sequential, and not all of the components will be needed in each lesson. [23] Here are the seven components, modified for library instruction purposes:

1. Anticipatory set—Activate prior knowledge of the students and engage them in the lesson.
2. Objectives—State lesson objectives at the beginning of the class.
3. Instructional input—Explain main concepts; use examples and visuals.
4. Modeling—Teacher demonstrates skills while students follow along.
5. Monitoring—Check for understanding and engagement throughout the lesson. Adjust instruction if needed and reteach if necessary.
6. Guided practice—Students answer questions or problems posed by the teacher or engage in group discussion or practice skills. Teacher gives feedback and checks for understanding.
7. Independent practice—Students work on their own to complete assignments, projects, or homework.

Other models are more specific and may include components such as materials required, time required, prerequisite skills, evaluation of student learning, and follow-up evaluation of the lesson with notes for instruction improvement.

Another useful model for library instructional design is the ADDIE model. [24] This model incorporates five phases of the design process:

- Analysis
- Design
- Development
- Implementation
- Evaluation

During the analysis phase, the instructor gathers information, reflecting on existing user skills and user needs. A formal needs assessment may be conducted. In the design phase, instruction is broken into learning objectives and an outline of instruction steps or a lesson plan is created. Activities for student engagement are considered. Next, during the development phase, instructional materials are selected or created and instructional strategy is mapped out. Finally, the session or course is implemented, and instruction is carried out as planned.[25] It is important to include an evaluation of the instruction session in order to assess the success of the planned instruction, whether it is a quick poll of the students at the end of an in-person session or a quiz that measures achievement of learning objectives. As part of the evaluation phase, plans for improving instruction can be created.

Steven Bell and John Shank have modified the ADDIE model specifically for academic librarians, creating the Blended Librarians Adapted ADDIE Model (BLAAM).[26] The steps in this model are:

- Assess users' needs and develop problem statement.
- Develop clear, measurable objectives.
- Design prototypes, implement plans, create materials needed for instruction.
- Deliver instruction.
- Measure how well the identified objectives were met.

Instruction in libraries is typically user focused by default. Academic faculty members will usually provide specific learning objectives for a library class. While planning is important, a successful teacher stays flexible and adjusts presentations and activities based on feedback from learners during the lesson. Assessment takes place throughout a teaching session. An assessment can be done at the beginning of the session by asking students about prior knowledge or having them take an interactive poll. Objectives may need to be adjusted based on the actual assessment of students' prior knowledge.

## CREATING LEARNING OBJECTIVES

Learning objectives use action words (verbs) to define what you want students to learn. They are active statements that describe specific sets of behaviors students should be able to perform after a program of instruction. Creating learning objectives helps to focus instruction sessions and facilitates assessment activities. Objectives should be shared with students, making the class goals and expectations clear. Bloom's taxonomy, specifically of the cognitive domain, can be used to help formulate learning objectives. There are many resources online for creating learning objectives from Bloom's taxonomy. For example, the International Assembly for Collegiate Business Education (IACBE) has produced an online manual describing Bloom's taxonomy and how to use it to write student learning objectives. Table 2.1 provides a sampling of active verbs that might be used to write learning objectives for each of the levels of cognitive processing from the simplest (knowledge) to the more complex levels or higher-order thinking skills (synthesis and evaluation).[27]

Depending on the target level of cognitive domain, learning objectives can be created that are actionable and assessable. Example learning objectives for an information literacy class could be "Students will be able to CHOOSE appropriate information sources" or "Students will EVALUATE Internet resources critically," depending on the level of processing appropriate for the level of the students and the course objectives.

## FOCUS INSTRUCTION ON THE LEARNER

Focusing instruction sessions specifically on the students and their specific needs is an important strategy for success. For example, when teaching a session on database searching, the librarian teacher could ask the course instructor or organizer of the session to help formulate a case that is appropriate to the group attending the session. During an introduction to evidence-based practice session for first-year medical students, you might use a case related to coursework they are currently covering in one of their core medical foundations courses, such as the use of childhood immunizations and their possible side effects. For medical residents, the usual practice is to address

**Table 2.1.**

| Cognitive Level | Sample Action Verbs |
| --- | --- |
| Knowledge | Acquire, define, group, identify, match, memorize, name, recognize, select |
| Comprehension | Associate, classify, describe, discuss, explain, give examples, interpret, recognize, rewrite, show, summarize, suggest |
| Application | Apply, choose, classify, differentiate, demonstrate, employ, experiment, interpret, investigate, model, present, produce, solve, use |
| Analysis | Analyze, classify, compare, contrast, criticize, debate, determine, differentiate, discover, examine, outline, transform |
| Synthesis | Arrange, build, compose, construct, create, derive, develop, invent, modify, produce, relate, synthesize, write |
| Evaluation | Appraise, argue, assess, critique, distinguish, evaluate, interpret, judge, rank, score, validate |

the resident groups by specialty; the chief resident can often give a real-life case example to use in the library presentation. Faculty members may also be able to provide a controversial or hot topic related to their discipline that will engage the students in a searching exercise and discussion of results. Asking a student to provide a topic during search demonstrations can be more challenging than a prepracticed search, but it also can be much more engaging for the students since it is often related to their research.

## ACCOMMODATING LEARNING STYLES

Whether or not individuals have different learning styles and how that affects teaching and learning is a topic of some debate among educators. Some generalizations can be made without going to the extent of labeling students as one type of learner or another. Also, students may learn in more than one way depending on the situation and subject. Richard Felder and Linda Silverman in 1988 created a model that divided learners into two main groups: active experimenters and reflective observers.[28] It may be that people use both of these methods of learning, but one mode may be dominant. Active learners feel comfortable experimenting, while reflective observers are more comfortable with introspection. Reflective learners may need to have more time to think about and process information than active learners. Time for thinking and organizing thoughts needs to be built into instruction in order to accommodate more-reflective learners. Also, active learners may be more comfortable doing group work, whereas reflective learners prefer to work alone or with a single partner. Felder and Silverman also wrote that different teaching styles might be of greater benefit to students using one or the other learning style.[29] Giving students choices and mixing up instructional methods can help accommodate all learners. It makes sense to include both active learning and reflection in classroom sessions to benefit all kinds of learners.

## PLANNING FOR INSTRUCTION

In order for library instruction to be student centered and address specific learning objectives, it is important to coordinate with faculty members before instruction, especially if the session is not embedded into the curriculum and occurs only one time. This is often called the "one-shot" session. Faculty members often will approach a librarian to teach a one-shot library session during the course of the semester without clear guidelines on what will be taught and how it integrates into his or her course. Sometimes the instructor will be absent during the library session. It is not necessarily a deal breaker if the instructor will not be present, but these sessions are less likely to be successful, especially if students are not required to attend. Having the course instructor present at a library session gives context and continuity to the session, and often the instructor will add information, which backs up the librarian's authority and can clarify how the students will use the information being presented.

One technique that librarians know well, the reference interview, can also be useful in planning for instruction. The reference interview can be used with faculty members in order to get the information you need for a successful one-shot instruction session.[30] One of the most important things to find out is how the library session is related to the work the students are currently doing in the course. Relating the session directly to student research or to a specific class assignment will guarantee that the students will be more engaged with the session since the session will present crucial information they will need to know in order to complete a class assignment. Giving students class time to actually work on the assignment after presenting information can also be a very successful and engaging model of instruction.

Carol Kulthau's stages of information finding can be used to ascertain the stage students will be at during a research project in order to help focus an instruction session on specific student needs.[31] Kulthau breaks down a research project into several stages. For information literacy instruction purposes, these stages can be abbreviated into three research steps:

1. Initial search for a research topic and refining of the search
2. Focused searching once a topic is decided on
3. Post-search citation management

Depending on where students are in the research process, the library instruction session can be focused on helping them complete the assignments they are currently working on and anticipate next steps. Sessions given at the beginning of a course before research has begun are less successful because students have less motivation to engage with the lesson. Just-in-time instruction is the goal, and librarians should negotiate with faculty to give presentations when most needed by the students.

Beyond the timing of the library instruction session, it's also important for presession planning to find out how many students will be attending, whether or not computers will be available if needed, and any prerequisite knowledge the students will already have gained. Getting a copy of the course syllabus and research assignment will go a long way toward helping library instruction align with course objectives and focus on specific skills students need in order to complete course assignments. Best practice is to have a face-to-face conversation with the faculty member to discuss the assignment and objectives. The library instructor can then create an outline for the session and send it to the faculty member, who can provide feedback to tailor the session to the specific needs of the class. This usually takes very little time, helps reduce the guesswork in planning, and can give the library instructor more confidence going into the session.[32] Library sessions can sometimes be difficult because the librarian is a "guest speaker" in the class and does not have much time to get to know the students and build a relationship. Engaging students by asking questions and getting feedback on their specific needs can help. Talking with the instructor about course objectives before the session also helps librarians build professional relationships with faculty members, who begin to view librarians more as equal partners in the educational process.

## EMBEDDING LIBRARY INSTRUCTION IN THE CURRICULUM

Traditional one-shot instruction sessions clearly will not provide students with the in-depth research skills needed for success in today's information-intensive work environments. Curriculum-based instruction is the answer to the need for librarians to be more integrated into academic disciplines in order to provide just-in-time instruction as well as providing multiple sessions for students as they progress in the acquisition of information skills. Increasingly, librarians are being asked to collaborate with faculty in designing courses, coteaching in discipline-based courses, facilitating problem-based learning sessions, and designing stand-alone, for-credit courses taught in person or online.[33] The library liaison role or embedded librarian model typically involves librarians spending more time in the academic department. It's common for librarians in this role to teach both students and faculty as well as serve on curriculum committees and attend departmental meetings.

## DIRECT AND DISCOVERY INSTRUCTION METHODS

Instruction can be divided into two different types of strategies: direct instruction or discovery instruction.[34] Both methods are useful to library instruction depending on the material and objectives of the class. Direct instruction is the more traditional method, where the instructor lectures or leads a class through a demonstration. Discovery instruction follows the constructivist school of thought; the instructor acts as a guide, setting up and facilitating problem-based learning. Library instructors will often use both methods in one session; for example, in a one-shot instruction session, library databases can be demonstrated and then students can have time for hands-on searching, guided by the librarian, who then helps individual students as needed. Any mode of instruction where the students are not actively participating can be classified as direct instruction. This includes lectures, demonstrations, panel presentations, static online web guides, and noninteractive video tutorials. Examples of discovery instruction include interactive tutorials where the learner has the opportunity to choose content, a discussion or debate, group projects, problem-based learning, and gaming.[35] While both direct and discovery methods can be used successfully, it is important to remember that higher-order thinking skills are being used in discovery learning and students will be more engaged with that method. Using direct instruction when time is limited and using discovery instruction when there is ample time for exploration is a good rule of thumb.

To be successful with direct instruction, the teacher must have clear goals for the session, check for understanding while giving instruction, and provide closure at the end of the session.[36] This process can be expanded to the following more-specific steps:

- State the objectives of the learning session.
- Review prerequisite knowledge the students should have already.
- Present new material or demonstrate techniques.
- Pose questions to assess learner comprehension.
- Provide time for practice.
- Assess learning and provide feedback.
- Review the course objectives and give examples of future application of the material.

The direct instruction method works very well for traditional library sessions and has sound pedagogical backing, although it is not as interactive as the discovery method. Depending on the situation and the preferences of individual teachers, each method can be used successfully for library instruction.

## PRESENTATION SLIDES—TO USE OR NOT TO USE?

When planning a library session, it is a good idea to create at least a general outline of the session when planning for instruction. The outline or lesson plan can be shared with the instructor before the lesson and adjusted for the needs of the specific class. Some librarians, especially when new to teaching or when teaching a subject that is unfamiliar, will create a script for the entire session. It can be helpful to plan an entire session in this way, but be cautious of following the script too closely and losing engagement with class attendees. Also, be prepared to veer off the script if need be. Asking questions at the beginning of the class to check for prior knowledge will help direct a session. Hopefully, in the pre-planning stages, the faculty member requesting the session provided good information about the students and their needs so there will be no surprises to deal with during instruction. Checking for comprehension as the class session proceeds is also important. You may need to veer from the script to reteach something that was not clear to all students.

LibGuides or library webpages can be used as examples during a presentation and then students can refer back to them after the session as they work on their research. Preparing handouts with a general outline of the material or process covered, including librarian contact information for follow-up questions, can be a good strategy.

Longer presentations for which there are no corresponding webpages or presentations where the Internet may not be available may require the creation of slides for the audience to follow visually. While a picture is said to be worth a thousand words, there is controversy around the use of PowerPoint or other slide-creation software and how effective (or ineffective) this method of presentation can be. In a study of PowerPoint and how it relates to educational methods, the authors found that students often report they learn more when slides are shown during a presentation.[37] Although PowerPoint is ubiquitous in business, education, and training today, there are critics who feel it is at best misused and at worst "making us stupid."[38] The positive effects of using computer-generated slides during instruction include increased engagement with the material and benefits to human learning derived from combining visual with verbal information. Students overwhelmingly agree in multiple studies that PowerPoint slides help organize course materials and note taking and improve their learning of the material.[39] Negative effects of using computer-generated slides can occur if the slides include too much textual information or flashy graphics that distract the viewer from the material being presented rather than enhancing the material. Also, PowerPoint slides can be used excessively, decreasing student-teacher interactions, which are also important to learning outcomes. Slides can also be made available online or through a content management system (CMS) for students to review later.

## TYPES OF LIBRARY INSTRUCTION

Librarians are involved in a growing variety of instructional programs across their institutions. Information literacy instruction is the traditional curriculum that librarians have been involved with for many years. Students are traditionally taught research, searching, evaluation of resources, and citation management, as well as avoiding plagiarism. Medical librarians are increasingly involved in teaching evidence-based practice and research methods in addition to traditional database-searching classes and workshops. The full spectrum of scholarly publishing from traditional publishing models to open access and data management is also being taught by some academic librarians. In first-year experience programs, librarians partner with academic faculty to introduce new students to an array of subjects that will increase their success in college and ease their transition to college life, including information literacy skills. Depending on the institution, librarians can be involved as guest lecturers in one-shot sessions arranged by a faculty member, as co-teachers of a series of sessions for a course or program, as teachers and coteachers of for-credit courses, and as teachers of entire sections of campus-wide integrated programs, such as first-year experience courses. At some institutions, librarians may be involved in all of these types of instruction.

## Information Literacy Instruction

In the book *Teaching Information Literacy Threshold Concepts*, the authors set out to identify the key concepts that all students need to know in order to be information literate. Threshold concepts are defined as representing "a transformed way of understanding, or interpreting, or viewing something without which the learner cannot progress."[40] These concepts, once identified, can then become learning objectives, and lesson plans can be created for teaching the core concepts. The Association of College and Research Libraries (ACRL) Framework for Information Literacy, mentioned in chapter 1, can also be used to identify core objectives. It is up to individual librarians to create instruction sessions that effectively communicate these core ideas in engaging and meaningful ways. Threshold concepts identified from the ACRL framework include[41]

1. scholarship as conversation,
2. research as inquiry,
3. authority is constructed and contextual,
4. information creation is a process,
5. searching as strategic exploration, and
6. information has value.

The ACRL website has suggestions on how to implement and use the framework and encourages faculty-librarian collaboration in planning and implementing information literacy instruction. Threshold concepts such as the concepts in the ACRL framework are difficult to teach effectively in on-shot lecture sessions. Since librarians do not often get the chance to teach full courses, it is imperative that we work with faculty to make sure library instruction is integrated into the curriculum at the point of need.

## Websites for Information Literacy Instruction

- ACRL Information Literacy Resources—www.ala.org/acrl/issues/infolit
- ACRL Introduction to Information Literacy—www.ala.org/acrl/issues/infolit/intro

- Big 6 and Higher Ed—http://big6.com/pages/lessons/articles/big6-and-higher-ed-information-seeking-strategies-and-library-instruction.php
- *Information Literacy* blog—www.informationliteracy.org.uk/blog/
- LibGuides Community—http://libguides.com/community.php (search for "information literacy")
- Library Orientation Exchange (LOEX)—www.loex.org/
- MERLOT Library and Information Sciences—http://libraryandinform ationservices.merlot.org/
- Project Information Literacy—http://projectinfolit.org/

## Medical Education

"Competencies for Lifelong Learning and Professional Success," the educational policy statement of the Medical Library Association (MLA) published in 2007, acknowledges that the work environment of medical librarians is particularly challenging.[42] The document lists professional competencies that health sciences librarians need for success. Competency number 6 states that health sciences librarians should "understand curricular design and instruction and have the ability to teach ways to access, organize, and use information."[43] Specific knowledge proficiencies include adult learning theory, educational assessment, instructional methodologies, and management of educational services. Curriculum design and instruction is also mentioned as a crucial skill. The document states that "an essential responsibility of the health sciences librarian is to teach ways to access, organize, and use information to solve problems."[44] Topics that health sciences librarians teach range from general information literacy and PubMed training, to evidence-based practice, systematic reviews, and clinical research databases. Libraries that serve hospitals and clinics also have the added complication of specialized instruction to practicing medical personnel, which is often done outside of the library in conference rooms and other meeting places, which may or may not have technology set up for presentation or practice. Because of the complicated environment in medical libraries, the MLA is committed to providing a wide variety of continuing education courses for practicing medical librarians.

## First-Year Programs

In an interview with a learning services librarian at Virginia Tech, an innovative program was described that explored library engagement within a first-year writing course.[45] First-year experience programs are intended to help freshman college students transition from high school and engages them in on-campus activities and educational programs. Library instruction was already integrated into the program at Virginia Tech, but librarians wanted to try new methods in order to maximize impact and move beyond the traditional one-shot session. They piloted four new teaching approaches in order to explore new ways of engaging with students to compare with the traditional approach. One new approach was to create a series of drop-in research studios where any student from any section of the course could meet with a librarian for a personal consultation. The highest attended sessions were those scheduled near the end of the course, right before a research paper was due. Another approach was to have students play a game where partners collaborate to complete a series of research tasks that mirrors tasks they need to learn to complete the course objectives. Another approach that was very successful was flipped classroom workshops, which required students to watch a video and complete a short assignment before coming to class and practicing what they learned with a librarian present to encourage deeper processing of the concepts. The fourth approach was to provide support and training for course instructors who wanted to integrate library concepts into their own classrooms. For all of the methods, librarian collaborations with faculty members were found to be key to successful learning experiences for students. A toolkit was created for teams of librarians who worked together to teach multiple sections of the class. The toolkit included sample lesson plans, video tutorials, and worksheet handouts. Graduate student teachers especially appreciated collaborating with a librarian to teach information concepts.[46]

## ASSESSING INSTRUCTION

Some form of assessment should happen with every instruction session. There are many ways to collect feedback. A survey or poll can be created and given at the end of the class. Instructors can have students write a quick one-page statement detailing what they learned and giving feedback on the session. Anecdotal feedback can also be solicited from students at the end of the class. Assessing whole instruction programs should also be done, as needs and participants change. Methods for assessing instruction programs could include surveys, focus groups, or anthropological observation. There are two types of evaluation methods: summative and formative. These two methods of assessment should be used together for a full picture of the effectiveness of instructional programs. Methods of evaluation are grouped into summative or formative evaluation depending on when they take place in the learning process.[47] Formative assessment is done during the learning process and can be repeated as the process continues. Formative assessment also helps the instructor assess how the students are progressing, and adjustments to instructional content can be made if necessary. Summative assessment is done at the end of instruction, whether it be one session or an entire course.

This measurement is meant to show how much learning occurred, thus show-ing the effectiveness of the instruction. Optimally, summative assessment occurs some extended time period after the end of instruction as well as immediately after instruction in order to show long-term retention of the material. One way of measuring long-term retention of skills is standardized tests. Some academic institutions have begun measuring the success of col-lege programs by administering the National Survey of Student Engagement (NSSE) test. While library-related questions are not asked on the main sur-vey instruction, there is an add-on module that measures information literacy experiences.[48] The 2015 information literacy module asks students to com-ment about their use of information sources, knowledge of scholarly commu-nication issues, and effective use of information.

Librarians know that library instruction teaches students skills that are crucial for career success and lifelong learning, such as information literacy, problem solving, and critical thinking. The problem is how to convince our institutions that this is true and get them to invest in libraries and library instruction programs. Assessment is crucial to proving our worth and im-proving instruction programs. Assessment takes many forms, and it is impor-tant to choose the right method at the right time. Descriptive statistics—for example, numbers of instruction sessions completed—are not enough to jus-tify the worth of library programs. According to a 2012 study of the best methods for evaluating the educational impact of library programs, the most common type of assessments in libraries are affective measures.[49] These types of assessments measure student attitudes about library teaching and services. While these measures are important in order to know how students feel about libraries, they do not provide an accurate measurement of student learning. Students often overestimate their own knowledge. Methods of di-rectly testing student knowledge and demonstrated learning provide better evidence of learning than asking students how much they feel they have learned. Practical demonstrations of student learning, such as being able to search effectively, are the best measures of actual learning. These measure-ments of student performance could take the form of exercises like perform-ing a search, answering a clinical question, simulations involving problem solving, case analysis, project results, research papers, or portfolios of stu-dent work.[50]

## IMPROVING LIBRARY INSTRUCTION PROGRAMS

In a 2005 study of college teaching practices, the author reports that while librarians get very little training in instructional methods and practices during their MLIS coursework, academic faculty also do not get enough formal training in teaching methods while pursuing their graduate work. Both new academic faculty and librarians rely on mentoring from colleagues, on-the-job training, and workshops on instruction in order to develop and improve their teaching practices.[51] Some ways that colleges and universities are improving instruction programs that also apply to library instruction include peer assessment programs, teaching portfolios, and in-house training programs. Peer assessment programs can be voluntary or tied to promotion and tenure. Peers do classroom observations and provide written feedback to junior faculty. Teaching portfolios are a collection of teaching materials, evaluations, and reflections on practice from individual instructors or an entire instruction program. While peer assessment and teaching portfolios are relatively new ways to improve and assess instruction, institutional workshops and training programs are more common. It is important for the administrators at an institution or library system to develop a "culture of teaching" in order to promote continued improvement of instruction programs. Some institutions have created teaching and learning centers on campus as part of an emphasis on improving instruction across the entire institution.[52] As librarians become more involved in teaching information literacy across the curriculum, in first-year programs, and in interdisciplinary subject areas, we can become full partners in teaching and learning at our institutions.

Some librarians will be more comfortable in the instructor role than others depending on personality and skill set, but everyone can develop better skills with practice. The best teachers are those with experience who have developed the ability to tune in to their students and adjust their methods to emerging needs in the classroom while they are engaged in teaching. Observing student reactions, asking for feedback, and checking for comprehension are all important behaviors of effective teachers. Just like learning any new skill, such as riding a bike or playing a musical instrument, learning to teach can be a trial-and-error process. Doug Lemov, an author of popular books on teaching, feels that teachers need to practice teaching in order to become more effective teachers rather than just learning about teaching methods. He emphasizes that "you can't learn if you are afraid to fail." Both teachers and students need to be open to failing and accepting suggestions for improvement, which they then put into practice.[53]

Because of the importance of library skills to college success and lifelong learning, emphasis needs to be put on developing effective library instructional programs and marketing them to the institution or community. Due to incorrect images of librarians and the work they do, a public relations effort may be needed before librarians are seen as full partners with faculty in educating students for successful jobs and careers. In an article on the image and role of the librarian, the author found that students often had no idea of the level of skill needed to become a librarian or the type of work librarians do in educational institutions.[54] Faculty and students should be made aware of librarian education, skills, and publishing record so that perceptions of the role of librarians can be changed and librarians can be seen as partners in educating students in our communities, schools, and institutions of higher learning.

Librarians need to see themselves as key partners in the information age, and then faculty and students will also see librarians as key partners. Focusing less on the library as a place and more on the expertise of librarians is an important shift that needs to happen and will be recognized more as librarians move out of the library space and become more integrated and embedded in schools, academic departments, clinics, and the community. Including information on librarian background, research, and expertise on websites and course management systems will also help improve the image of librarians. Above all, practicing teaching and bringing your own style and personality to the classroom will go far toward creating a positive image of library instruction at your institution, and faculty will begin to see you as a valuable partner in educating students. Students will see you as an important source of valuable information and as someone who can positively impact their future careers and life goals.

## WEBSITES AND BLOGS FOR TEACHING LIBRARIANS

- *ACRLog*—http://acrlog.org/
- *American Association of School Librarians* blog—www.aasl.ala.org/aaslblog/
- Blended Librarian—http://blendedlibrarian.learningtimes.net/
- *Designer Librarian*—https://designerlibrarian.wordpress.com/
- Edutopia (K–12)—www.edutopia.org/
- te@chthought—www.teachthought.com/
- *Pumped Librarian*—http://pumpedlibrarian.blogspot.com/
- *The Ubiquitous Librarian*—http://chronicle.com/blognetwork/theubiquitouslibrarian/

## HELPFUL BOOKS FOR LIBRARIAN TEACHERS

- Blevins, Amy, and Megan Inman. *Curriculum-Based Library Instruction*. Lanham, MD: Rowman and Littlefield, 2014.
- Booth, Char. *Reflective Teaching, Effective Learning: Instructional Literacy for Library Educators*. Chicago: American Library Association, 2011.
- Bravender, Patricia, Gayle Schaub, and Hazel McClure. *Teaching Information Literacy Threshold Concepts: Lesson Plans for Librarians*. Chicago: Association of College and Research Libraries, 2015.
- Buchanan, Heidi E., and Beth A. McDonough. *The One-Shot Library Instruction Survival Guide*. Chicago: ALA Editions, 2014.

- Eden, Bradford Lee. *Enhancing Teaching and Learning in the 21st-Century Academic Library*. Lanham, MD: Rowman and Littlefield, 2015.
- Farmer, Lesley S. J. *Instructional Design for Librarians and Information Professionals*. New York: Neal-Schuman Publishers, 2011.

## NOTES

1. Steve Kolowich, "Study: College Students Rarely Use Librarians' Expertise," *AASL Hotlinks* 10, no. 6 (2011): 1.

2. Ibid.

3. Jennifer Howard, "What Matters to Academic Library Directors? Information Literacy," *Wired Campus* (blog), accessed July 30, 2015, http://chronicle.com/blogs/wiredcampus/what-matters-to-academic-library-directors-information-literacy/51005.

4. Scott Walter, "Librarians as Teachers: A Qualitative Inquiry into Professional Identity," *College & Research Libraries* 69, no. 1 (2008): 51–71.

5. Howard, "What Matters to Academic Library Directors?"

6. Antonio DeRosa and Marisol Hernandez, "Trends in Medical Library Instruction and Training: A Survey Study," in *Enhancing Teaching and Learning in the 21st-Century Academic Library*, edited by Bradford Lee Eden (Lanham, MD: Rowman and Littlefield, 2015), 43–57.

7. Ibid.

8. DeRosa, "Trends in Medical Library Instruction."

9. Jason Sokoloff, "Information Literacy in the Workplace: Employer Expectations," *Journal of Business & Finance Librarianship* 17, no. 1 (2012): 1–17.

10. Ibid.

11. American Library Association, "JobLIST," accessed July 30, 2015, http://joblist.ala.org.

12. John D. Shank, "The Blended Librarian: A Job Announcement Analysis of the Newly Emerging Position of Instructional Design Librarian," *College & Research Libraries* 67, no. 6 (2006): 514–24.

13. Ibid.

14. Ibid.

15. M. Walker Buckalew, *Twenty Principles for Teaching Excellence: The Teacher's Workbook* (Wilmington, DE: Independent School Management, 1992).

16. Ibid.

17. Barbara J. Millis, "Active Learning Strategies in Face-to-Face Courses," Idea Paper 35, IDEA Center, accessed July 31, 2015, http://ideaedu.org/wp-content/uploads/2014/11/paperidea_53.pdf.

18. Ibid.

19. Ken Bain, "Popular Teachers and Great Ones," *REDU: Revista de Docencia Universitaria* 10, no. 1 (2012): 11–14.

20. Ibid.

21. Bradley C. Greiman and Mary Anne Bedtke, "Examining the Instructional Planning Process Taught in Agricultural Education Teacher Preparation Programs: Perspectives of University Faculty," *Journal of Agricultural Education* 49, no. 4 (2008): 47–59.

22. Ibid.

23. Ibid.

24. Jessica Cole, "Instructional Roles for Librarians," in *Curriculum-Based Library Instruction*, edited by Amy Blevins and Megan Inman (Lanham, MD: Rowman and Littlefield, 2014), 3–10.

25. Lesley S. J Farmer, *Instructional Design for Librarians and Information Professionals* (New York: Neal-Schuman Publishers, 2011).

26. Ibid.

27. International Assembly for Collegiate Business Education, "Bloom's Taxonomy of Educational Objectives and Writing Intended Learning Outcomes Statements," accessed July 31, 2015, http://iacbe.org/pdf/blooms-taxonomy.pdf.

28. Richard M. Felder and Linda K. Silverman, "Learning and Teaching Styles in Engineering Education," *Engineering Education* 78, no. 7 (1988): 674–81.

29. Ibid.

30. Heidi E. Buchanan and Beth A. McDonough, *The One-Shot Library Instruction Survival Guide* (Chicago: ALA Editions, 2014).

31. Ibid.

32. Ibid.

33. Cole, "Instructional Roles for Librarians."

34. Char Booth, *Reflective Teaching, Effective Learning: Instructional Literacy for Library Educators* (Chicago: American Library Association, 2011).

35. Ibid.

36. Ibid.

37. David G. Levasseur and J. Kanan Sawyer, "Pedagogy Meets PowerPoint: A Research Review of the Effects of Computer-Generated Slides in the Classroom," *Review of Communication* 6, nos. 1–2 (2006): 101–23.

38. Edward Tufte, "PowerPoint Is Evil," *Wired*, accessed July 31, 2015, http://isites.harvard.edu/fs/docs/icb.topic1276296.files/Session%206%20/Tufte_2003_Powerpoint%20is%20Evil.pdf.

39. Levasseur, "Pedagogy Meets PowerPoint."

40. Patricia Bravender, Gayle Schaub, and Hazel McClure, *Teaching Information Literacy Threshold Concepts: Lesson Plans for Librarians* (Chicago: Association of College and Research Libraries, 2015).

41. Association of College and Research Libraries, "Framework for Information Literacy for Higher Education," accessed July 31, 2015, www.ala.org/acrl/standards/ilframework.

42. Medical Library Association, "Competencies for Lifelong Learning and Professional Success," accessed July 31, 2015, www.mlanet.org/pdf/ce/200705_edu_policy.pdf.

43. Ibid.

44. Ibid.

45. Brian Matthews, "Library Engagement with First Year Writing: 4 Strategies: An Interview with Julia Feerrar," *The Ubiquitous Librarian* (blog), accessed July 31, 2015, http://chronicle.com/blognetwork.theubiquitouslibrarian/2015/07/12/.

46. Ibid.

47. Katherine Schilling and Rachel Applegate, "Best Methods for Evaluating Educational Impact: A Comparison of the Efficacy of Commonly Used Measures of Library Instruction," *Journal of the Medical Library Association: JMLA* 100, no. 4 (2012): 258.

48. National Survey of Student Engagement, "Topical Module: Experiences with Information Literacy," accessed July 31, 2015. http://nsse.indiana.edu/pdf/modules/2015/NSSE%202015%20Experiences%20with%20Information%20Literacy%20Module.pdf.

49. Schilling, "Best Methods for Evaluating Educational Impact."

50. Ibid.

51. Scott Walter, "Improving Instruction: What Librarians Can Learn from the Study of College Teaching," *ACRL Twelfth National Conference* (2005): 363–79.

52. Ibid.

53. Katrina Schwartz, "Why Teachers Should Be Trained like Actors," *KQED News*, accessed July 31, 2015, https://ww2.kqed.org/mindshift/2013/07/01/teaching-as-acting-a-performance-profession/.

54. Jody Fagan, "Students' Perceptions of Academic Librarians," *Reference Librarian* 37, no. 78 (2003): 131–48.

*Chapter Three*

# Teaching beyond the Classroom Walls

As libraries become more digital, there is less need for people to visit the physical library building to get access to resources. The library space can still be the hub of the community, where people meet, study, access computers, and use library services, but remote access to resources extends the reach of the library to community members who may be physically unable to visit the library. Online access to library resources also extends the community of library users from the local population to a global community. This access is provided virtually, reaching an extended community of users beyond the library walls. Librarian teachers also have a role in reaching out to their community members who do not physically visit the library. A virtual library learning space can take many forms. In this chapter, we will discuss ways to reach learners in virtual spaces, beyond the walls of the library classroom or computer lab, using new technologies for teaching and learning. Librarian teachers can provide information and teach library skills online in many different ways. In order to be effective online teachers, librarians need technology skills but also must have the knowledge, skills, and ability to effectively teach at a distance. In this chapter, we will consider the implications of distance teaching and learning as well as the librarian's role.

Teaching virtually is quite different from face-to-face teaching. Interpersonal cues are not present, and the teacher needs to find ways to acquire input from distance students in order to personalize instruction. Finding ways to make distance learning interactive can also be a challenge. Basic pedagogy and teaching skills used in face-to-face teaching also apply in virtual instruction, but teaching practices need to be tailored to the unique online learning environment. Like it or not, technology influences the learning environment greatly. Online learning environments have been improving since their introduction a couple decades ago, but they are still in need of improvement.

Librarians with skills in the areas of online web design, course management systems, web conferencing, and distance teaching methods are in high demand. Distance education is growing and promises to revolutionize education, especially in bringing higher education to areas of the world where skilled teachers may not be available locally.

There are several terms used to describe online learning. *Distance education* was historically the term used to describe the first mode of reaching learners at a distance. Originally, distance education was provided by sending mail-order instruction materials to students who signed up for "correspondence courses."[1] With the rise of the World Wide Web and spread of Internet connectivity, *online learning* has emerged as a common method of teaching and learning. Another term that is commonly used is *e-learning*, which can encompass any kind of electronic learning, including online and learning with multimedia such as CDs and video. More about multimedia learning will be presented in the next chapter. *Online learning* and *e-learning* are often used interchangeably. In this chapter, we will focus on learning with online technology and the pedagogy that makes this kind of learning effective and beneficial to students and instructors.

## TEACHING AND LEARNING WITH ONLINE TECHNOLOGIES

Online learning has obvious benefits for distance learning but can also be a more effective and efficient way to learn in some cases. Compared to the traditional classroom model, online or e-learning allows learners to be more in control of their own learning pace and process. Also called *web-based learning*, e-learning encompasses both distance learning and computer-based instruction in a classroom.[2] *Blended learning* is another form of instruction, which combines online learning with classroom instruction. Some benefits of e-learning for students include control over pace, sequence, and content focus, as well as the ability to learn anywhere at any time that is convenient. Benefits to instructors include standardization of content across multiple course sections, ease of updating content once it is created, automatic assessment and tracking of student progress, and the ability to create and update content anywhere, anytime. Online learning has been shown to be more interactive, catching the learner's interest and increasing his or her motivation to learn more. Increased retention and use of content as well as higher achievement has been demonstrated in studies that compared e-learning with standard classroom instruction. Other studies have shown that students actually prefer online learning in many cases.[3] In addition, well-designed online instruction organizes information for more efficient learning, easier review of materials, and modularization of content in order to break down information into smaller, more manageable concepts.

The core component of online learning is the "learning object." Learning objects are digital-content instructional items that can be reused and combined to facilitate e-learning.[4] Learning objects can be created to contribute to one or more student learning objectives. The advantage of e-learning objects is that they are modular and can be reused. Once they are created, they can be plugged into multiple learning environments, adapted and updated for use in multiple ways, and even added on to face-to-face learning to make it more interactive. Online learning can be learner directed or instructor led.[5] Learning objects can stand alone in self-paced instruction sessions or be used as one of several activities presented in instructor-led sessions. Self-paced instruction is best used for competency-based education when students are learning specific skills and competencies that must be mastered by the end of the program of study. Students have the flexibility to learn at their own pace and relearn concepts that prove challenging. Instructor-led sessions can be synchronous or asynchronous, but the instructor controls the order of the learning objects that are presented and multiple students are introduced to the same content at the same pace. Opportunities for interactions between instructor and students as well as between students enhance this kind of learning, making it more conducive to higher-order thinking and the development of critical-thinking skills.

Just like classroom teaching, online instruction should be based on learning objectives and organized through lesson planning. The same steps apply when teaching an online session, including gathering content, delivering instruction, and assessing learning. The main difference in online learning is the method of instruction delivery. Rather than face-to-face lectures, content must be delivered via computer-based content management systems or other technologies for creating web-based learning objects. Systems for online content delivery can range from simple websites to online portals and full-featured learning management systems (LMS). In addition, communications from the online instructor and between online class participants can be delivered synchronously in real-time through an online webinar or chat session or asynchronously through online forums and blogs. Standardization of online content delivery and accessibility can be addressed by using an Advanced Distributed Learning (ADL) sharable content object reference model (SCORM)–compliant LMS.[6] This ensures that content can be shared between different LMS and also student assessment systems. Using an LMS is also desirable because of the built-in accessibility tools as well as the ability to organize and reuse the content easily. Whichever method of presenting online learning is used, teachers have the ability to reach many more students, using the same content, than in face-to-face learning.

## NEW TOOLS FOR ONLINE INSTRUCTION

The rise of new learning technologies over the past few decades has enabled this huge growth in online learning. In addition to being used for distance education, online learning can also be used to augment traditional classroom courses. When online learning is combined with face-to-face instruction, it is referred to as *blended learning* or *hybrid* courses. The 2015 *Horizon Report* lists the increased use of blended learning as one of six top key trends in higher educational technology.[7] The report cites statistics from the U.S. government showing that one in ten students is enrolled in online courses. Clearly, this technology has become widely accepted by students. The report lists the benefits of adding online learning to traditional face-to-face instruction as increased flexibility and ease of access to materials, facilitation of the use of multimedia as well as synchronous and asynchronous tools, and allowing for better communication between instructor and students as well as facilitating discussions between students. To be successful, instructors using online learning must be able to create opportunities for social learning and stimulate critical-thinking processes through the use of online teaching technologies. Using multiple online tools to allow students to engage with concepts in multiple ways will also help to allow for different student learning preferences.

Tools for online instruction have grown exponentially. Besides LMS, many free or inexpensive tools for interactive, cloud-based online learning and collaboration have appeared in the past few years. Just a few of the many innovative new online tools currently available for use in facilitating interactive online education include:

- Poll Everywhere—Respond to interactive online polls via a computer or smartphone (www.polleverywhere.com).
- VoiceThread—Upload slides, add voice-over, and share content with others (http://voicethread.com).
- SoundCloud—Upload, record, and share sounds online (http://soundcloud.com).
- Adobe Connect—Host online web conferences, share files, chat, and present interactive polls (www.adobe.com/products/adobeconnect.html).
- Screencast-O-Matic—Record a computer screen or from a webcam and share online (www.screencast-o-matic.com).
- Google Docs—Create shared documents and presentations and share with others (www.google.com/docs/about/).
- Google Hangouts—Online video chat with groups (https://hangouts.google.com).
- Skype—Video conference, share screens, and send files to anyone for free (www.skype.com).

- Edmodo—Enables sharing between teachers, students, and parents; post and grade assignments online (www.edmodo.com).
- Remind—Send automatic e-mails to students and/or parents without using a personal e-mail account (www.remind.com).

These tools can be used to add interactive online activities to any learning experience—face-to-face, blended, or online instruction. Many are available for free or can be obtained through institutional licensing or consortiums.

## THE GROWTH OF ONLINE EDUCATION

Each year since 2002, in partnership with the College Board, the Babson Survey Research Group has conducted a survey on the use of online education in the United States. The year 2013 marked the 11th annual report from the Babson Survey, showing the changing usage of online education for over a decade.[8] Responses were gathered from over 2,800 colleges and universities. When the report began in 2002, less than half of all institutions surveyed agreed that online education was critical to their long-term strategy. In 2013, 66 percent agreed that online learning was crucial and an all-time low of only 9.7 percent felt that online education was not critical to their institutional strategy (see figure 3.1).[9]

The Babson study also reported that 74 percent of institutions surveyed believe that online learning is as good or better than face-to-face instruction. An interesting finding is that even with decreasing enrollments in colleges across the nation, enrollments in online courses continue to grow. The survey reports the number of students enrolled in one or more online educational courses to be 7.1 million students, with 33.5 percent of students in the United States taking at least one online course.[10] This trend indicates a continued growth of online education, at least at most U.S. institutions of higher education. When the Babson Survey began in 2002, over 40 percent of the respondents felt that learning outcomes for online learning were inferior to face-to-face instruction. In 2013, only 26 percent still felt that online learning was inferior. The improvement in the quality of online instruction may account for some of this change, but there is clearly still room for more improvement. The survey also shows that while overall college enrollments are plateauing, online enrollments continue to rise (see figure 3.2).[11]

## EFFECTIVE ONLINE INSTRUCTION

The benefits of online instruction or e-learning include the convenience of learning anywhere at any time, flexibility and personalization of learning, and reduced cost to institutions, which can then serve more students with less

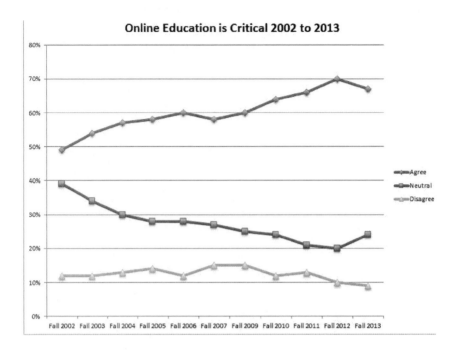

**Figure 3.1.    Percent of institutions believing online education to be critical (Babson study, 2013)**

staff expenses. [12] Since online instruction involves the use of technologies not necessarily used in regular face-to-face classroom instruction, training and support are needed for faculty to be successful in this new environment. Some research has been done to identify effective methods of teaching online, but there is still more work to do. When designing programs for delivering online courses, it is important to select the technology that best meets the needs of the institution and students. Depending on the scope of the program, compatibility with existing systems and cross-institutional collaborations should be considered as well as standardization. Technical support for software maintenance as well as troubleshooting issues encountered by instructors and students should be a crucial consideration. Building in an online help system or orientation to the LMS will help with the successful implementation of a new system. [13] It is also important that instructors get the training they need in order to effectively create and conduct online learning without feeling frustrated or held back by technological issues.

Including multiple ways of learning as much as possible within an online learning environment is good pedagogical practice. Both synchronous and asynchronous activities should be built into online courses. For example, in addition to asynchronous activities such as watching a video or posting com-

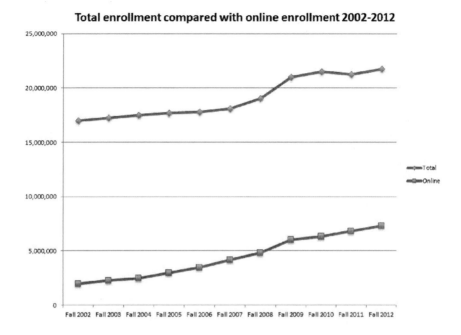

**Figure 3.2.   Changes in total and online enrollment (Babson study, 2013)**

ments on a discussion board, synchronous activities such as web-conferencing presentations or synchronous group discussions using software such as Google Hangouts should also be included. Communication methods are particularly important to online learning since students often do not have direct access to the instructor. Studies suggest that multiple methods of communication should be used, such as chat, discussion boards, web conferencing, formal instructional presentations, posting work for instructor feedback, and opportunities for students to reflect on assignments and materials.[14] In addition, interaction between participants in a course must be facilitated by the instructor. Interaction is an important feature of effective online learning. Designers of e-learning courses must learn new ways to facilitate higher-level discussion among the course participants in the online environment. It is also important to be aware that some students may have language barriers or need accommodations for effective learning that might not be as apparent in an online environment.

We have seen that online instruction continues to grow at a rapid rate, but there are often limited guidelines for instructors wanting to offer an online course. Some large benchmarking projects have been done, especially in European countries, in order to work toward frameworks for improving e-learning. In a 2011 report on quality in e-learning, the authors identified several criteria for creating and evaluating online learning.[15] These criteria can be applied to individual online courses to improve their effectiveness. Complex evaluation models have been created, but on a basic level there are ten important components to quality e-learning systems that have been identified:

1. Quality content
2. Structured environment
3. Facilitation of communication
4. Cooperative learning and interactivity
5. Assessment of student work
6. Flexibility and adaptability of the system
7. Tech support for students and instructors
8. Fully qualified instructors
9. Instructional leadership support
10. Appropriate allocation of resources to the program

Understanding student experiences and preferences in e-learning is also important for successful online teaching. In a 2010 survey, the authors reported on a sampling of students from many universities across Austria.[16] Students responding to the survey showed clear preferences for online learning in some situations and face-to-face learning in others. Online learning was preferred for providing a clear structure for learning, allowing for individual regulation of learning pace, and providing efficient access to learning materials. Face-to-face instruction was preferred for developing interpersonal relationships. Students preferred face-to-face learning when specific skills needed to be acquired or applied and online learning for self-paced instruction. Students were favorable overall about online education in spite of clear preferences for face-to-face learning in some situations. As technology improves and communication between instructor and students as well as among students is enhanced, then e-learning should become more acceptable in all situations. Moving beyond merely disseminating information online toward more interactive instructional methods, including offering real-world examples, opportunities for applying knowledge, and timely assessment of learning with immediate feedback, will improve the online learning experience for students.

## ONLINE INSTRUCTION IN LIBRARIES

In an article on designing information literacy courses for distance learning, the authors point out that students enrolled in distance learning courses are entitled to the same services as traditional students are able to obtain from the library, such as access to all resources and information literacy instruction. Further, in planning for distance learning education, libraries may be left out of the strategic-planning process for institutional distance learning initiatives.[17] Since skills taught by information literacy instruction, such as how to think critically about information, are crucial to creating lifelong, independent learners, it is important that the library be included in the educational experience for all students. Furthermore, online library instruction may also be more convenient for students in face-to-face classes that meet in the evenings. Some instructors prefer to assign online library instruction for homework instead of using class time. Access to online learning systems add flexibility to library programs, allowing librarians to choose the most effective methods for different situations.

Dewald and colleagues point out that in order to design engaging online instruction that features active learning, the type of technology used must be chosen carefully in order to fit the instructional need. Since contact with the instructor and with other students is crucial to engaging students, communication technologies are very important. Both synchronous and asynchronous communication technologies can be used to enhance online learning depending on the needs of the students and the particular course objectives.[18] Becoming familiar with all of the technologies available is important in deciding which technology will best suit the particular course needs. In a full-semester course, both synchronous and asynchronous technologies may be used together for a variety of instructional needs. For example, librarians assisting with research projects within an online course may decide to schedule synchronous chat sessions with students at crucial points in their research process in order to answer questions or help to refine research topics. Using online discussion boards allows students to interact with each other and with the instructor, building relationships and enhancing learning through social interactions and idea sharing. Asynchronous technologies such as online tutorials may be more appropriate for one-shot instruction sessions where database searching is demonstrated or other skills are practiced by students on their own at a time convenient for them. Tutorials can also be repeated, if needed, to review or relearn complex topics at the point of need. Best practices for web-based tutorials include building in interactivity, making them meaningful to the students' lives and current assignments, giving immediate feedback on learning assessments, and providing practice of skills learned as well as time for reflection on learning.[19]

Rita-Marie Conrad and J. Ana Donaldson in their book about creating engaging online learning recommend several key elements to ensure engaged learning in online environments.[20] They recommend that students be involved in some way in establishing their own learning goals, and that they should be enabled to work in groups. Students should be engaged by exploring resources to answer questions that are meaningful to them, and they should be involved in completing authentic, real-world tasks. Assessment must be ongoing, and assessment products should be shared with a wider audience, if possible, in order to add value to the greater learning community. Several conditions need to be present in order for engaged learning to be optimized. The learning strategy should be fully described to the students so they can partner with instructors, and many opportunities for communication about the learning strategy should be provided. Instructors should make expectations of participation and engagement clear to online students. Feedback on performance should be clear, as well as ways to improve performance. Opportunities for student self-assessment should also be provided. The instructor should endeavor to make the students feel that the online environment is safe and student centered, just as in a face-to-face classroom. Also, students who are new to the online environment will need support from the instructor to be able to fully interact and collaborate using the online tools available. [21]

## FACULTY PERCEPTIONS OF ONLINE EDUCATION

In a 2014 survey of faculty views on technology, *Inside Higher Ed* found that the majority of faculty respondents viewed online learning experiences as inferior to face-to-face courses. Most faculty members felt that meaningful interactions between students and teacher were missing from most online courses. Only a quarter of respondents felt that online courses could be equal to face-to-face instruction. [22] Problems that faculty identified as most lacking in teaching online courses included a reduced ability to answer student questions, less interaction with students, and less ability to identify and reach "at-risk" students. They were also concerned about delivery of content to meet learning objectives, lack of interaction with students outside of class, communications about grading, and communication about course logistics, as well as other issues. Faculty who had taught at least one online or blended course tended to rate online education as more equal to face-to-face learning, although most still considered online education to be lower quality. Most of the faculty in the survey who had not taught an online course either had never been asked or were not interested in teaching online. [23] In order to feel motivated to teach online, faculty felt they needed more professional development and training, and they also felt that online teaching needed to be more valued for promotion and tenure. Clearly, improved technology and more training programs are needed in order for faculty to fully embrace online teaching. This may conflict with their administration's desire to move more courses online and with student demand for more flexible course offerings.

# TECHNOLOGIES THAT ENABLE ONLINE EDUCATION

## Flipping the Classroom

A new method of teaching and learning that leverages the power of online learning to augment face-to-face instruction is called *flipping the classroom*. In this blended instructional model, prerecorded lectures are posted online for the students to view on their own time. Classroom time is reserved for group discussion and other active learning assignments. Active learning has been shown to be positively associated with increased student learning outcomes. With the rise of free tools and course management systems that make it easy to record and post video lectures online, flipping the classroom has become an easy and effective way to make face-to-face learning more interactive. Studies have shown that student performance improves with online video lectures over in-class lectures, although shorter videos are preferred. Posting lectures and worksheets online and reserving class time for active learning also led to performance increases in several studies. [24] While college students don't always complete homework reading assignments, studies have shown that they do watch video lectures assigned for homework. Flipping the classroom is one way to move away from lecture-based, instructor-centered learning toward a more student-centered and active learning approach. The LMS is often used to enable the flipped classroom.

## Course and Learning Management Systems

Software for enabling online learning is referred to as *course management systems* (CMS) or *learning management systems* (LMS). These terms seem to be used relatively interchangeably. CMS software scaffolds online learning by presenting all of the information students need to learn a particular subject or competency in an organized and sequential way. It includes tools for facilitating learning and communication with students as well as assessment of learning. Some commonly used LMS software includes: Moodle, Canvas, and Blackboard. Blackboard is particularly popular, and a July 2015 Reuters article stated that the Blackboard platform was for sale and could sell for up to 3 billion U.S. dollars. [25] Canvas is a competing LMS that is increasing in popularity and includes built-in modules to help organize learning. The Canvas tools seem very intuitive for both instructors and students. Moodle has been around for a while now and is free for anyone to download and set up on a web server. Some institutions create their own in-house LMS if they have computer programming staff available to take on a project of this size. Keeping the software updated and adding new features also take a lot of staff time, so many institutions prefer to purchase a system and pay the support costs rather than invest staff time and effort.

In a 2015 Educause report in partnership with the Bill and Melinda Gates Foundation, the authors survey the current status of LMS and call for the next-generation digital learning environment (NGDLE) tool to bring LMS to the next level.[26] Currently, LMS are not keeping pace with the changing needs of higher education, which calls for an even more student-centered approach to learning. While almost 100 percent of higher education institutions have an LMS, not all of the faculty use it, and only 56 percent use it on a daily basis. About 83 percent of students today use an LMS for one or more courses. Although many faculty and students are using this technology, many are dissatisfied with its capabilities. The Educause study found that 15 percent of institutions planned to replace their LMS within three years. Also, of the faculty using an LMS, relatively few use the more advanced features, such as those allowing interaction outside the classroom. The most common use of an LMS is for administrative tasks such as distributing materials and posting online grades.[27] A more student-centered model focused on enabling higher-order thinking and learning is what is needed for the future.

The Educause report on the NGDLE calls for a new standard of online learning systems that are personalized, accessible, interoperable, and that incorporate assessment, analytics, and collaboration tools. These new tools would be personalized for the student and instructor and would also be able to be personalized at the district or consortium level. Since one system cannot provide all the components needed for this kind of system, the report calls for developing new standards so that developers can create programs that plug into the LMS and extend it. For example, there are already learning modules and apps in existence that could be added on as software plug-ins to provide content or tools for learning. Students and instructors would be able to add new content or tools just like plug-ins are added to web browsers such as Firefox. The technology that will enable this to be possible is described as being like Legos, with the interlocking mechanisms being standard programming that allows the tools to be used with each other.[28] Furthermore, the development of the NGDLE will begin with accessibility for all students instead of having to add accessibility as an afterthought. Learning analytics will be a key component to the NGDLE, allowing students and instructors to customize learning to actual needs, integrating extra content and assessment as needed, automatically. Instruction analytics can also be collected and used to improve instruction methods. Another area for development is integrating planning and advising systems into the LMS. These types of programs already exist but are not integrated into existing LMS at this time. Finally, competency-based education, which is growing in popularity, focuses on the acquisition of specific skills rather than completion of a whole course. Next-generation learning systems should be flexible enough to allow for multiple approaches to learning, from competency-based learning to traditional, course-based learning.[29]

An even more futuristic ideal for the NGDLE is to provide the opportunity for students to collect their work in online portfolios that persist over their academic careers. Standardization could also make it possible for a student to transfer work seamlessly from high school to college. The current generation of LMS is only accessible by private login due to copyright reasons and for the privacy of student work and grades. A more modularized system would allow for part of the system to be private while the rest of the system could be open to a larger learning community beyond the institution. Open educational resources (OER) are also important in this future learning environment. Since OER provide content that is open access and freely available to use and reuse, password protection is not as necessary and education becomes more open.[30] Mobile apps could also be plugged in to this future system if they use the same interoperability standards that enable the system to work with multiple plug-ins. Some examples of work toward this future learning environment include Instructure (Canvas) Mastery Gradebook (www.canvaslms.com/news/press-releases/instructure-unveils-learning-mastery-gradebook), which enables competency-based online education; EdCast (www.edcast.com) personal knowledge network; Acatar (www.acatar.com) course translation services; Instructure's Edu App Center (www.eduappcenter.com), which provides a collection of plug-in tools for Canvas; and Brightspace LeaP (www.brightspace.com/products/leap), an adaptive learning system that customizes the learning experience to student preferences. Accessibility standards are also being developed, as is adaptive technology that could work with online learning systems and enable online education to be more accessible to students with disabilities.

## Social Media and Distance Learning

Web 2.0 tools and social media can be used with distance learning in order to create a highly personalized learning environment for students. The authors of a 2012 article on social media and self-regulated learning, propose a three-step framework for helping students use social media in order to take control of their own learning online.[31] At the basic level, instructors provide students with access to blogs or wikis where they can organize their learning activities by creating calendars, writing in journals, or saving bookmarks, files, or videos related to their learning activities. At the second level, students are guided to use the social features of blogs and wikis in order to give and receive feedback from other students and to collaborate on group projects. At the third level, students are guided to use higher-order reasoning skills, such as synthesizing information by engaging in self-reflection and evaluation of their learning process and planning for improvement, using web 2.0 social media tools. With this model, social media tools are used to scaffold student learning and encourage students to take ownership of their own learning process, as well as to give them tools to organize their learning for a course. A wide variety of social media tools, including ones the students are already using, such as Facebook and Instagram, could also be used along with blogs and wiki software.

## OER

Open educational resources (OER) are an important development that can be used for augmenting online education. The idea of OER has arisen with other open access movements such as open access journals. Due to the high cost of textbooks and lack of materials for online courses, some faculty have begun to develop their own online textbooks and courses, which they share with other faculty in online educational communities such as the Multimedia Educational Resource for Learning and Online Teaching website, also known as Merlot II (www.merlot.org).[32] On Merlot, a student can search for open access textbooks on many subjects or find videos and other teaching materials to augment those used in their courses or to learn a new subject on their own. Faculty can find textbooks, video tutorials, readings, and even full course modules that other educators have posted as freely available to download and modify for their own use. Merlot II currently has over 40,000 items from participants around the world. Many educational institutions and organizations list their open educational resources on the OER Commons (www.oercommons.org), which currently contains over 50,000 items that are freely shared to other educators under a creative commons license that allows them to be repurposed, modified, and adapted for educational needs.[33] Some items require the user to give attribute to the creator, and some restrict use to noncommercial purposes.

## MOOCs

Massive Open Online Courses or MOOCs are another open educational movement. MOOCs are large-scale online courses with learning objectives related to a specific subject or area of study presented in an online format with readings, assignments, lectures, and tests.[34] Students from anywhere around the world can sign up to take an MOOC as long as they have an Internet connection. Theoretically, MOOCs are free, but some have associated fees if offered for credit or a certificate. Typically, MOOCs are offered by larger institutions that can afford to experiment with new technologies. Partner organizations such as Coursera, EdX, Futurelearn, and Udacity have arisen to offer online learning platforms where well-known faculty from large universities can record their lectures and reach a worldwide audience. Coursera is arguably the most well known in the United States, while Futurelearn is a newer MOOC platform from the United Kingdom. EdX has a worldwide audience. Some larger higher education institutions are now also experimenting with directly offering MOOCs from their own platforms.[35] Stanford University was one of the original universities to experiment with offering an online course in artificial intelligence. Over 160,000 people from over 190 countries enrolled. Udacity is the expanded result of that original successful experiment. Udacity offers what it calls *nanodegrees* in technology-job-related subjects.[36] Smaller institutions with tight budgets and an emphasis on small classrooms with more faculty-to-student interaction are typically critical of MOOCs. One of the major criticisms of MOOCs is that the course completion rate is very low. While students of all ages from around the world are able to enroll in MOOCs, statistics show that most drop out before completing the course.[37]

In an effort to improve the delivery of online education, including MOOCs, Google is sponsoring research by Carnegie Mellon University that is looking into ways to automatically provide feedback to large numbers of students in online environments, create better social networking in online courses, and make online education more responsive to a variety of cultural backgrounds.[38] Researchers are hoping to make large online courses more engaging in order to unlock the potential to reach students around the world. It is hoped that more engaging online courses will improve retention and open up worldwide access to education. One benefit of current MOOCs is that they generate a lot of data about large numbers of students from many different demographics. Analyzing this data could help to improve online pedagogies. The Carnegie Mellon University researchers are looking at ways to improve retention in MOOCs by offering socialization activities and group assignments. Ways to make the content more engaging and entertaining, such as incorporating game play, are also being explored. Computer programs are being developed to personalize the online student experience by automatically identifying the level of subject mastery, providing feedback or additional instruction when needed, and skipping over mastered subjects to new material.[39]

The Babson study shows that despite the buzz about MOOCs and their potential to revolutionize education, adoption of this technology is extremely low.[40] Only about 3 percent of higher education institutions offered MOOCs in 2013, when the study was completed. Only about 9 percent had plans to offer MOOCs in the future. These numbers had grown only very slightly from the year before.[41] Typically, only the largest institutions with over 15,000 students enrolled have begun offering MOOCs on an established basis. In the Babson study, the top reasons institutions gave for adopting MOOCs included increasing institutional visibility, driving student recruitment, exploring innovative pedagogy, offering flexible learning opportunities, and reaching new students. One early promise of MOOCs was that they might provide a way to reduce educational cost, but the technology has obviously not advanced to that stage as yet. Many of the institutions surveyed that had experimented with MOOCs did not find them to be sustainable. One major outcome that could come of experimentation with MOOCs is enhancements to online education as a whole due to studies carried out on the large amounts of data collected from these courses.

## GLOBAL ONLINE EDUCATION

In an article on online learning and social responsibility, the author makes the case for encouraging online learning due to its potential to make access to education available to underserved populations.[42] Online learning in this case refers to learning using Internet technologies where instructors and students can be in any location at any time. Global online learning puts the control of the learning experience fully in the students' hands. This in turn makes education more accessible for some populations of students that are underserved by traditional educational models. Some examples include those with physical handicaps who have limited mobility, those who live in remote geographic areas where education is unavailable, those who cannot afford or do not desire to leave their communities where education is either not available or where the educational program they desire is not available, as well as those who need more rigorous coursework than is available in their community. Online education also opens up continuing educational opportunities to working men and women, military personnel, or mothers with young children who cannot attend traditional courses during the day. Incarcerated individuals or those with psychological challenges who cannot attend courses in traditional face-to-face classrooms also have increased access to educational opportunities with online education. Besides accessibility, online education that includes people from many backgrounds, cultures, and geographic locations can break down cultural and interpersonal barriers, increasing understanding and cooperation between sociocultural groups. Online learning opens up the educational experience to any age group and therefore encourages lifelong learning.[43] By bridging social divides and connecting disparate communities in educational conversations, online education can help build a more inclusive global society for the future.

The British Open University is a good example of an institution striving to make education accessible to everyone worldwide. The Open University admits people from all ages and backgrounds. In fact, there are no formal admissions requirements for many courses. Because of the flexibility of the Open University model and the use of accessibility technologies, the university claims to enroll more disabled students than any other European university. Currently, over 12,500 students with a range of disabilities, including mental health issues, are enrolled. The Access Centre provides services such as computer software or personal assistance in order to enable disabled students to fully participate in the university.[44] The Open University also targets underrepresented populations and offers extra support to help them succeed. Free Open University content is available anywhere an Internet connection can be found through iTunes U, YouTube, the OpenLearn website, and Open Research Online, with over 15,000 open access research publications. The British Open University has been a leader in international education for over 20 years, working in partnership with governments and governmental organizations to provide educational training in countries that do not have access to education, especially in health care, teacher education, and English-language training. This training can be done for free by using OER and Internet-enabled educational platforms.

## BEST PRACTICES FOR ONLINE TEACHING AND LEARNING

In an article reporting on a project to identify good teaching practices online, the authors studied a 2004 book by Ken Bain, which reported observations of "what the best college teachers do." After interviewing and observing over 60 teachers identified as outstanding through their awards and reputation, Bain identified some of the characteristics that made these educators so successful.[45] Many of the things that make face-to-face education successful can also be applied to online learning. In this model, teaching is more of an art form than a science. The outstanding teachers identified by Bain were able to foster deep learning, a desire to learn more, and many times a fundamental change in the student's worldview. Teachers studying Bain's work reported on a project to identify online best practices and common themes for exemplary online education. Best practices identified included facilitating student interaction and involvement in the course, organizing course materials well, building a teacher presence online, and clearly conveying expectations for students.[46] Beyond best practices, it was found that the best online college teachers foster student engagement by encouraging students to be reflective, actively fostering student motivation, and creating a sense of community by incorporating social learning. Lecturing should not be the primary method of delivering educational materials, rather the teacher's most important role is to foster a high level of interaction and participation as well as active learning.[47] In the online environment, videos, blogs, wikis, and discussion forums encourage active and social learning. Small-group discussions can be set up online and help to build a community of learners. Blogs, wikis, and cloud applications such as Google Docs can be used for reflective thinking on real-world problems and for collaborative projects among other activities.

Class content needs to stimulate intellectual development. One way that outstanding teachers foster intellectual development in their students, according to Bain, is to encourage students to ask questions and seek answers to those questions.[48] Problem solving is very important, but it is even more important to propose problems that are personally meaningful to students and that they are interested in solving. Online surveys and discussion boards are ways of determining the questions that students are interested in. Students who learn to ask questions and find answers become effective lifelong learners. Successful online teachers also need to build a genuine rapport with their students. They can do this in online courses by including background information and sharing personal experiences with their students. Introductory activities where the students get to know each other and their instructor better are important for fostering rapport and building an online community. The online teacher also needs to be present for students, solicit questions, and be available for help when needed.[49] Online instructors should address students by name, give personal feedback, and adapt the course to individual student needs, just as they would in a face-to-face setting. Using the available technology and adapting it to fit good pedagogy and the learning needs of individual students can be the key to successful online teaching.

## ASSESSMENT METHODS FOR ONLINE LEARNING

Good online assessment of student learning, like assessment in traditional settings, should be based on course objectives. If the course is focused on learning particular skills and knowledge building, multiple-choice questions may be appropriate. There are many ways to create multiple-choice questions for evaluating learning online. Many CMS have multiple-choice-question builder modules built in. Using online polling software such as Poll Everywhere allows a quick poll of students' knowledge before, during, or after a learning session for an informal check for comprehension or to test for prior knowledge. Course content can be adjusted based on the results of the poll. Informal, anonymous polling is a good way to add active learning to a class session, and students can answer quickly from their computer or phones. Results are shown immediately in the poll results window. This is a fun and popular activity, and students have no fear of getting the "wrong" answer since it is informal and anonymous. LibGuides also have a basic multiple-choice polling option built in that can be used for informal polling. Other ways to build quick, effective online multiple-choice quizzes for either formative or summative assessment include using Google Forms or Qualtrics surveys, as well as many other free survey- or quiz-making tools available online.

Many online courses, including information literacy courses, may involve higher-order learning skills, such as evaluating and synthesizing information. When assessing applied knowledge and critical-thinking skills, multiple-choice questions may not be the best way of assessing learning. In this case, measurement of learning can best be done by providing authentic, real-world problems for students to solve individually or in groups.[50] Problem solving can be scaffolded online through a CMS or website, which provides steps to be taken in the problem-solving process. Students should also be allowed time to reflect on problem solving. This can be facilitated online by journal writing or discussion boards. Problem solving is a student-focused activity that measures learning but also helps students to develop critical-thinking skills and improve their learning processes. The focus is on the process and not the final outcome, so grading may need to also be focused on the process rather than on a final exam. Self-assessment of learning is another activity that encourages students to reflect on the learning process and make plans for improvement. Creating online portfolios of student work can be a method of assessment that also allows for student self-reflection as skills increase. In problem-solving activities, students can create process logs where they write out the steps they take or, in the case of information literacy instruction, the search strategies they used.[51] In the same way, research logs can be kept, documenting the steps taken in the research process. Course grades can be based not only on the final research paper but on the quality of the research process, and feedback can be given along the way to improve learning.

## CREATING ONLINE LEARNING MODULES

The creation of online learning modules can be time consuming and challenging, especially for those attempting to convert a face-to-face course to a fully online course. Hybrid courses, where some sessions are face to face and other content is organized and presented online, may provide the best of both worlds. For courses that are offered fully online, reaching out to students in distant parts of the world or even to nearby students who are not able to come to campus for regular classes, video conferencing may be the answer to providing face-to-face interaction at a distance. Creating separate modules and testing them one at a time before putting them all together to create a full course may be a good strategy. Using good pedagogy and choosing technology tools carefully while keeping a student-centered focus will ensure a successful online course.

Whether you want to add asynchronous, online learning to a face-to-face course, teach an online course module, or are using a hybrid model, there is much to be gained by teaching online. Benefits for teachers include the reusability of online course modules, tools for the organization of course materials, and ease of updating materials. For students, good online instruction can foster independent learning skills, higher-order thinking, and lifelong learning skills, as well as provide the convenience of learning anytime, anywhere. The benefits far outweigh the effort required to learn a new method of teaching. Training is available through online courses, continuing educational programs, and often through the faculty learning centers that are becoming common on the campuses of many higher education institutions. For library instruction, which is often held outside of the traditional classroom, online teaching and learning is a perfect solution, backed by sound pedagogy and leading to increased student learning and teaching efficiency.

## NOTES

1. Joi L. Moore, Camille Dickson-Deane, and Krista Galyen, "e-Learning, Online Learning, and Distance Learning Environments: Are They the Same?" *Internet and Higher Education* 14, no. 2 (2011): 129–35.

2. Jorge G. Ruiz, Michael J. Mintzer, and Rosanne M. Leipzig, "The Impact of e-Learning in Medical Education," *Academic Medicine* 81, no. 3 (2006): 207–12.

3. Ibid.

4. Moore, Dickson-Deane, and Galyen, "e-Learning, Online Learning, and Distance Learning."

5. Ibid.

6. Ruiz, Mintzer, and Leipzig, "The Impact of e-Learning in Medical Education."

7. L. Johnson, S. Adams Becker, V. Estrada, and A. Freeman, *NMC Horizon Report: 2015 Higher Education Edition* (Austin, TX: New Media Consortium, 2015), accessed September 30, 2015, http://cdn.nmc.org/media/2015-nmc-horizon-report-HE-EN.pdf.

8. I. Elaine Allen and Jeff Seaman, "2013—Grade Change: Tracking Online Education in the United States," Online Learning Consortium, 2014, accessed October 3, 2015, http://onlinelearningconsortium.org/survey_report/2013-survey-online-learning-report/.

9. Ibid.

10. Ibid.

11. Ibid.

12. Heather Glynn Crawford-Ferre and Lynda R. Wiest, "Effective Online Instruction in Higher Education," *Quarterly Review of Distance Education* 13, no. 1 (2012): 11–14.

13. Ibid.

14. Ibid.

15. Ebba Ossiannilsson and Lena Landgren, "Quality in e-Learning—A Conceptual Framework Based on Experiences from Three International Benchmarking Projects," *Journal of Computer Assisted Learning* 28, no. 1 (2012): 42–51.

16. Manuela Paechter and Brigitte Maier, "Online or Face-to-Face? Students' Experiences and Preferences in e-Learning," *Internet and Higher Education* 13, no. 4 (2010): 292–97.

17. Nancy Dewald, Ann Scholz-Crane, Austin Booth, and Cynthia Levine, "Information Literacy at a Distance: Instructional Design Issues," *Journal of Academic Librarianship* 26, no. 1 (2000): 33–44.

18. Ibid.

19. Ibid.

20. Rita-Marie Conrad and J. Ana Donaldson, *Engaging the Online Learner* (San Francisco, CA: Jossey-Bass, 2004).

21. Ibid.

22. Carl Straumsheim, "Online Ed Skepticism and Self-Sufficiency: Survey of Faculty Views on Technology," *Inside Higher Ed*, October 29, 2014, accessed October 18, 2015, www.insidehighered.com/news/survey/online-ed-skepticism-and-self-sufficiency-survey-faculty-views-technology.

23. Ibid.

24. Jacob Lowell Bishop and Matthew A. Verleger, "The Flipped Classroom: A Survey of the Research," presented at ASEE National Conference Proceedings, Atlanta, GA, 2013.

25. Liana B. Baker, Greg Roumeliotis, and Mike Stone, "Exclusive: Education Company Blackboard Seeks $3 Billion Sale," Reuters, July 28, 2015, accessed October 15, 2015, www.reuters.com/article/2015/07/28/us-blackboard-providence-idUSKCN0Q226R20150728.

26. Malcolm Brown, Joanne Dehoney, and Nancy Millichap, "The Next Generation Digital Learning Environment: A Report on Research," Educause Learning Initiative, April 27, 2015, accessed October 15, 2015, www.educause.edu/library/resources/next-generation-digital-learning-environment-report-research.

27. Ibid.

28. Ibid.

29. Ibid.

30. Ibid.

31. Nada Dabbagh and Anastasia Kitsantas, "Personal Learning Environments, Social Media, and Self-Regulated Learning: A Natural Formula for Connecting Formal and Informal Learning," *Internet and Higher Education* 15, no. 1 (2012): 3–8.

32. Merlot II website, accessed September 13, 2015, www.merlot.org/merlot/index.htm?action=about.

33. OER Commons website, accessed September 13, 2015, www.oercommons.org/about.

34. Educause, "7 Things You Should Know about MOOCs II," Educause Learning Initiative, June 11, 2013, accessed October 15, 2015, http://www.educause.edu/library/resources/7-things-you-should-know-about-moocs-ii.

35. Ibid.

36. Udacity website, accessed September 13, 2015, www.udacity.com/us.

37. Educause, "7 Things You Should Know."

38. Byron Spice, "Google Sponsors Carnegie Mellon Research to Improve Effectiveness of Online Education," press release, Carnegie Mellon University, June 24, 2014, accessed August 27, 2015, www.cmu.edu/news/stories/archives/2014/june/june24_improvingmoocs.html.

39. Ibid.

40. Allen and Seaman, "2013—Grade Change."

41. Allen and Seaman, "2013—Grade Change."

42. Barbara L. Stewart, "Online Learning: A Strategy for Social Responsibility in Educational Access," *Internet and Higher Education* 7, no. 4 (2004): 299–310.

43. Ibid.

44. British Open University, "Mission," accessed September 14, 2015, www.open.ac.uk/about/main/mission.

45. Ken Bain, *What the Best College Teachers Do* (Cambridge, MA: Harvard University Press, 2011).

46. T. M. Brinthaupt, L. S. Fisher, J. G. Gardner, D. M. Raffo, and J. B. Woodard, "What the Best Online Teachers Should Do," *Journal of Online Learning and Teaching* 7, no. 4 (2011): 515–24.

47. Ibid.

48. Bain, *What the Best College Teachers Do.*

49. Brinthaupt et al., "What the Best Online Teachers Should Do."

50. Dewald et al., "Information Literacy at a Distance."

51. Ibid.

*Part II*

# Using Educational Technology to Scaffold Learning

*Chapter Four*

# Activating Learning with Multimedia

One of the most important goals of the librarian teacher is to encourage increased student engagement for better learning outcomes. Using multimedia in presentations and activities can be a way of engaging students of all ages. This is especially important when it comes to library instruction, which can often be viewed as less than exciting, making students less motivated to participate. It is important to engage students interactively in teaching and learning, especially when working with younger generations, who are used to rich media and technology in everyday life. Creating a learning environment where students have an active role in creating their own knowledge is the key to engagement. The use of multimedia technology tools in education can help teachers create instruction sessions that encourage students to actively participate in instruction. Multimedia can also be used to stimulate student creativity and initiate higher-order thinking and learning processes, such as critical thinking.

There are many different definitions of the term *multimedia*. It can be used broadly to include the use of pictures and graphics in instruction or more narrowly to mean text and graphics that can be viewed interactively in a digital form. For the purposes of this chapter, we will use the broader definition to explore the pedagogy behind the use of multimedia. Although multimedia can be used in teaching without the use of technology, we will also explore examples of the use of the interactive technology that enables active learning with multimedia. This definition of the use of multimedia in education includes common instruction activities such as teaching with live demonstrations of databases and websites, something that librarians do frequently. In this chapter, we will explore ways of making learning more engaging and interactive using multimedia and technology, moving beyond the one-shot, 50-minute database demonstration. The one-shot method of teaching can be highly interactive if the students are involved in doing live searching on topics they are interested in, as well as working in groups and using other techniques we have covered in previous chapters. This chapter takes the next step in extending interactivity through the use of multimedia technology, which can promote having the students take the lead in directing their own learning. In this case, the teacher sets up the learning environment but then steps back and becomes a guide for the students as they become creators of their own knowledge.

The 2015 *Horizon Report* (higher education edition) cites improving digital literacy as one of the most pressing challenges faced by educators today.[1] While students are using information technology and media in their daily lives, they do not necessarily know how to correctly use information in their academic lives. They need help from their teachers to learn to use technology and information sources critically and creatively in a scholarly fashion. While the integration of information technology is more common in K–12 classrooms, higher education lags behind and is faced with an increasingly technology-oriented student body who expect a technology- and media-rich environment. While schools may implement technology initiatives that provide funding to purchase computers and multimedia software or digital whiteboards and clickers for interactive teaching and learning, the key to using these technologies creatively in the classroom is to provide training for faculty members about how to use the technology effectively. Faculty support centers, in-service training, and helpful technology support staff are key to making technology initiatives successful. Teachers need to know how to leverage new technology in order to facilitate higher-order learning processes such as analyzing information and reflecting on learning.

## LEARNING WITH MULTIMEDIA

Many researchers have studied the effects of different types of multimedia on student learning. Studies on adding graphics to text-based lessons reveal that students report enjoying the lessons more when graphics are added. While any graphical addition to text can raise student engagement, only adding graphics that are appropriate to the instruction or that are instructive in themselves can improve learning. In fact, adding graphics that are not related to the instruction but that have a distracting value for students, such as pictures of famous people or unrelated animations, actually reduces learning as measured by post-tests after multimedia lesson modules are completed by students.[2] In other studies, adding graphics that have emotional appeal, such as using bright colors or displaying engaging animations, has been found to have a positive effect on learning for college-age students. Researchers hypothesize that appealing graphics motivate students to work harder and engage with the material more, thereby improving learning outcomes. [3] Again, it is important that the graphics are essential to the instructional material so that they don't distract from the lesson, which would reverse the positive effect of adding the graphics. Although adding graphics to text has been shown by researchers to have a positive effect on learning, the important points to remember when using any kind of pictures or multimedia include: reduce extra cognitive processing by avoiding distracting graphics or multimedia; use media that accurately represent the concepts being taught; and use graphics that are appealing to the learner and therefore motivate him or her to work harder on the lesson. Another important aspect of learning with multimedia involves breaking down lessons into manageable sections in order to avoid overloading cognitive processing. [4]

Stephen Bell advises using active learning methods in library sessions to combat "IAKT" or "I already know that" syndrome, which can be the attitude of some students attending library instruction. [5] Bell does traditional library database demonstrations but with a twist. He encourages the students to lead the demonstrations, talking them through the process but having students in the class volunteer to do the actual demonstration as their classmates observe. This method is not only interactive with the hands-on use of computer technology, but it quickly exposes what the students don't know about the subject. Bell admits that having students lead demonstrations can be risky, but he feels the benefits outweigh the chances of the session going in unexpected directions. The librarian can always take back control of the session, but getting the students directly involved is much more engaging. This is one way of making a lecture-based session more interactive if a lab with student computers is not available. In a computer lab, all of the students can follow along with the demonstration, which is a more optimum way of learning database searching. Bell advises talking to course faculty members before involving students in live demos as well as picking students carefully with the help of departmental faculty or picking students you already know. [6] This method of teaching is not for everyone but illustrates a creative and interactive use of multimedia technology that can be fun for the entire class as well as the instructor.

Many studies by educational researchers have shown that learning with multimedia increases learning outcomes. This is because presenting both text and pictures activates two separate parts of the brain, increasing cognitive processing. This is termed the *multimedia effect*. [7] In addition, studies have also shown an increase in long-term memory with the use of multimedia materials. Learning can occur from using just text or auditory input, but understanding has been shown to occur faster when visual information is added. Additionally, a picture can give more precise information about a subject that is not available in a text description, leading to better understanding and avoidance of misunderstanding. For example, an invalid mental model can be constructed from a text-only description of an object, whereas a picture of the object is less abstract and also gives more spatial cues to the viewer. Pictures and multimedia can be said to provide scaffolding for learning by helping to create mental models that support later processing and understanding of the text.[8] In other words, using multimedia will support quicker comprehension, more precise understanding, and future learning.

## TEACHING WITH MULTIMEDIA

Using multimedia when teaching visual subjects such as art, film, and design is a standard practice. Using slides, film clips, and other media are considered essential in these subjects. Multimedia can also be useful for fostering understanding when teaching science or social studies. For example, when teaching genealogy, showing the family tree provides a visual of the idea of generations and relationships. Social studies and humanities instructors can significantly enhance the learning experience by incorporating multimedia into the classroom to illustrate social concepts, to portray historical events, or to bring up controversial topics for discussion or debate.[9] Similarly, librarians could introduce news clips to illustrate controversial issues in scholarly communications in order to make the topic more relevant to real life.

Studies have shown that college students, especially non-majors, have trouble understanding the relevance of scientific subjects to their personal lives. When students are thus disengaged from the subject, less information is retained.[10] Besides trying to relate science to everyday life and therefore make it more relevant to students, studies have shown that the use of multimedia tools such as videos, games, or simulations can actively engage students and stimulate curiosity about the subject, which can then lead to a greater sense of relevance. Charles Prober and Salman Khan[11] propose the use of video instruction in education in order to teach basic science concepts more easily as well as consistently within and across institutions. Using video learning to construct the basic framework of scientific knowledge frees up time for instructors to focus on presenting a problem for discussion or facilitating team-based exercises that explore real-world cases taken from areas of faculty expertise. A library of basic knowledge videos could even be shared among institutions and centrally updated as subject knowledge changes. This would also free up time to conduct deeper learning on subjects that students are interested in pursuing as a research focus. Similarly, librarians can create reusable videos and other media that can be shared and reused for teaching basic knowledge and concepts needed for information literacy instruction to be shared within the institution or between institutions. Class time could then be used to explore and extend the concepts learned in the videos.

In another study on learning with multimedia in medical education, increased retention of information was seen with the use of multimedia compared to the traditional lecture format. Many educators use PowerPoint to augment lectures, but text-laden slides with long lists of bullet points are much less effective than using less text and augmenting it with illustrative pictures.[12] The pictures must be essential to understanding the information being presented or they risk adding "noise" that will decrease comprehension of the material. The process of using text and pictures together activates two distinct channels in the brain's processing system. Each channel has a limitation to how much information it can process. It is theorized that by using more than one channel, more information can be processed. This can work with auditory (lecture) information as well.[13] Science education especially uses both text and pictorial learning, mainly during the undergraduate years when teaching basic sciences and anatomy.

Richard Mayer has written a lot about the "cognitive theory of multimedia learning," which describes how people take in sounds and pictures and process them in order to create knowledge.[14] Knowledge of the cognitive process allows instructors to be able to facilitate deep learning by following good pedagogical practices and not overwhelming students with too much information or distracting them from key information, which is important for optimum learning. A fine balance needs to be maintained by providing enough information but not overwhelming the student while also challenging the student and providing motivation for continued learning. According to Mayer, best practices for creating multimedia lessons include:[15]

- removing extraneous text and graphics;
- highlighting material essential to the learning objective;
- locating accompanying graphics near to descriptive text;
- preteaching key concepts;
- creating short, learner-controlled sessions;
- providing voice-over with text material;
- using graphics with text for increased learning;
- using conversational speech rather than a formal tone; and
- using human speech rather than computer-generated speech.

Good instructional design is the key to successful teaching and learning with multimedia. Simply adding graphics to teaching materials will not improve learning. In a study on designing effective multimedia instruction using different instructional methods, the authors found that lesson design was much more important than the technology used by the student to complete the lesson.[16] College students were presented with the same multimedia tutorials on either a desktop computer or an iPad. One set of tutorials was a standard series of multimedia graphics illustrating a science topic. The other set of tutorials incorporated two new instructional methods that have been shown to increase learning.[17] The first method, segmenting, involves cutting the lessons into smaller segments by topic or idea. The second method, signaling, involves adding highlighting to multimedia objects in order to focus attention. The authors added headings to slides as well as controls so that students could spend as much time on each slide as was needed before progressing to the next slide rather than presenting the entire tutorial without being able to pause. The results of the study showed that while the technology used to present tutorials (desktop or iPad) was not a cause of increased learning, the instructional method (segmenting and signaling) was a significant cause of increased learning.[18] Students enjoyed using the iPads and were possibly more motivated to continue learning with the devices, but the technology was not a substitute for good instructional methodology.

## LEARNING STYLES AND MULTIMEDIA

Effective instruction also allows for different learning styles in individual students. Multimedia instruction needs to be student centered to allow for differences in preferred methods for working with multimedia learning objects. While the technology used to create learning objects such as slides, tutorials, videos, games, or simulations can be varied, the pedagogical methods for creating them should be based on sound principles. In a 2010 study on matching learning styles with learning objects, the author found that types of learners could be divided into categories that can be tested by style-inventory questionnaires.[19] Some people prefer one way of learning over another, whether it be aural, visual, textual, or kinesthetic. Most people are multimodal in that they highly favor two styles, sometimes more. As people age, they appear to be able to learn in more ways than very young students, but this may be due to the different ways in which they were taught while growing up. Learners can also differ in their preference for hands-on or reflective learning as well as sequential learning or a more holistic "big-picture" method. Some studies have also found cultural differences. One study reported that some Asian American students may prefer reflective, independent learning, while African American, Latino, and Native American students may prefer hands-on and group-oriented learning.[20] In the learning-styles study, college students from different cultural backgrounds were given a static webpage with screenshots, a video tutorial, and an interactive video tutorial after being tested for learning-style preferences. Regardless of preferred learning style, 80 percent of the students preferred the static tutorial because it allowed them to pause and try out the procedure before moving on.[21] They also liked that they could refer back to the tutorial later if they forgot the procedure being taught. While not as technologically advanced, the screenshot tutorial was designed in a way that allowed for multiple modes of learning and therefore appealed to more of the students. If time allows, producing learning objects in multiple formats and allowing students to choose their preferred media style could produce optimum student learning outcomes.

## TECHNOLOGIES FOR MULTIMEDIA LEARNING

### Using Clickers and Polling in the Classroom to Enhance Teaching and Learning

We have seen that multimedia educational materials are engaging to students, encouraging them to participate in creating their own knowledge. Multimedia technology can be used to promote active learning as recommended in the constructivist model of learning. Multimedia technology can also be used to facilitate higher-order thinking with class activities such as discussions, group projects, hands-on learning, and simulations. Higher-order cognitive processes such as solving problems, reflection, analysis, and evaluation are also engaged with the use of multimedia materials. In a 2011 study of active learning in library instruction, the researchers compared traditional lecture-style instruction with problem-based learning and the use of clicker technology.[22] Clickers allow students to respond immediately to an instructor's question by using handheld devices or computers. See figure 4.1 for an example of clicker technology. While no clear differences were found between the type of instruction and student scores on post-tests, students found the more active sessions using problem-based learning and clickers to be more engaging and enjoyable.[23] Students became more animated, and participation increased in the active learning sessions. Another advantage of using clickers in the classroom is that assessment questions can be integrated into lessons, allowing instructors to focus individual sessions on the specific needs of the class and to adjust sessions as needed to spend more time on concepts that students are not fully grasping.

Using clickers in the classroom is considered a form of multimedia instruction because student answers can be shown as results of polls and displayed in a graphical representation for all students to view. Studies have shown that using clickers is engaging for students, provides immediate feedback, and also provides assessment data.[24] Besides purchasing electronic clickers, online software for polling such as Poll Everywhere is also available. Students can respond from their laptop computers or a mobile device. Polling can be used to pose challenging questions from which a classroom discussion or problem-solving session can be facilitated and can be an easy way of adding interactivity to a traditional face-to-face class session. It can also be used to encourage students in the reflective process, which is very

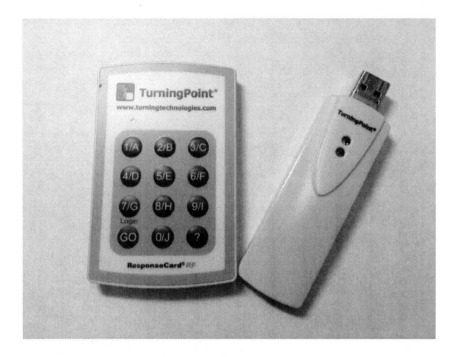

**Figure 4.1.   Clicker technology**

important to student learning outcomes. Because answers are anonymous, students may be less inhibited than when raising their hands, and participation can be increased. For best results, poll questions should be short, focused on learning objectives, and worded in conversational form without using jargon or needing additional explanation.[25] One example of the effective use of polling in the classroom is beginning a class session with a couple of poll questions about students' background or prior learning. The poll questions engage the students and also help give the instructor an idea of what concepts the students may or may not be familiar with so that the session can be customized to student needs.

## Using Electronic Whiteboards and Displays in Multimedia Education

Another interactive technology that can be used to facilitate multimedia learning is the electronic whiteboard. In the introduction to *The Cambridge Handbook of the Learning Sciences*, the author explains the power of educational technology to transform educational practices, stating, "Computer software is central to the learning sciences because the visual and processing power of today's personal computers supports deep learning."[26] Electronic whiteboards are a good example of this technological support of deep learning. Technology can support deep learning by representing abstract knowledge in concrete forms, allowing learners to communicate knowledge in visual ways, supporting reflection on learning, and allowing learners to revise knowledge as they learn.[27] Electronic whiteboards are able to offer this advanced support of learning through a combination of computer technology and supporting software. The ability to display multimedia presentations and physically interact with the board allows learners to develop a deeper understanding of the concepts being presented.

Electronic whiteboards have been in use in the business world since the late 1990s, and there is a growing body of research on their uses in education.[28] Most of this research has been carried out in elementary and secondary school educational settings, but they are also used in higher education and business settings. An electronic whiteboard, or interactive whiteboard, is a large whiteboard connected to a computer and projector. The whiteboard is sensitive to touch and can be marked up with special pens. Text or drawings made on the board can then be saved to the attached computer's hard drive to be printed or distributed by e-mail. Most electronic whiteboards come with custom software that allows for the creation of interactive presentations. Notes that are written on the board can be saved to a file to be shared with a group. There are several manufacturers of these electronic boards, and they range in price from a couple thousand dollars to tens of thousands of dollars. Some of the same effects can be achieved from connecting a computer to a wall-mounted TV screen, which can be cost effective but doesn't include the software that makes the technology truly interactive.

Electronic whiteboards promote student learning by engaging students. Some learning theories that can be identified with interactive whiteboards include constructivism, active learning, and whole-class teaching. Their large size facilitates collaborative group projects and the interactive component fosters active learning. Electronic whiteboards have also been used to make learning more accessible to visually or physically impaired students.[29] Some of the many uses of interactive whiteboards include demonstrating computer applications and Internet sites, saving the results of a brainstorming activity or class discussion, display of color images and graphics, combining sound and visuals when learning a foreign language, manipulation of numbers in a visual manner in mathematical education, and support of distance learning by capturing lecture content.[30]

In a study of the use of electronic whiteboards in the United Kingdom, the authors found that most research studies done on interactive whiteboards were overwhelmingly positive but were based on mostly teacher and student opinions using surveys, interviews, and questionnaires.[31] These studies were informal, and little information was given on the research methods used, making it hard to extrapolate global findings of benefit to teacher education. However, two main categories were studied in these reports from the UK whiteboard project: enhancing teaching and supporting learning. Potential benefits for teaching and learning were identified as flexibility of the whiteboards in the classroom, enabling multimedia presentations, support for development of teaching resources, ease of modeling computer-use skills, promotion of student interactivity, and encouragement of participation in lessons.[32] Although this study did not find any evidence for increased student achievement, there was a clear preference by teachers and students for the use of electronic whiteboards. Training and support were big issues, and the authors found that usage of the boards was sometimes limited to writing on them as on traditional, nonelectronic whiteboards, without transforming classroom practices at all, due to lack of teacher training in using the technology effectively in the classroom. The authors call for further research on teaching and learning with interactive whiteboards and on understanding how technology and teaching practices intersect.

William Beeland, technology coordinator at Trinity College in Dublin, conducted a survey of teachers' and students' attitudes about the use of interactive whiteboards in classrooms.[33] Through the use of a questionnaire created for measuring attitudes toward technology, Beeland found that the use of interactive whiteboards in the classroom led to increased student engagement due to the visual learning aspect of using the board. Faculty members in the study found it easier to move away from traditional lecture modes of teaching toward more of a facilitator role when using the electronic whiteboard and encouraging students to use the board as well. Student attention levels were increased when using the board due to the visual and hands-on aspects of activities. In a large study at South Texas Community College (STCC), Starr County Campus, 609 students were surveyed about the amount of use and perceived educational value of several types of educational technology, including electronic whiteboards. The researchers found that the students believed that having technology in classrooms helped them learn, even if that technology was not used.[34] The highest rating of usefulness of equipment in this study was for electronic whiteboards. The use of educational technology by instructors was found to be so variable that no guiding principles of usage were found. Students at STCC also expressed frustration with the lack of availability of educational technology. The authors concluded that further study of instructors' knowledge and attitudes toward educational technology is needed in order to keep up with student needs and expectations.[35]

*Using Interactive Whiteboards in Library Instruction*

Library computer labs are an obvious place for colleges and universities to pilot the use of electronic whiteboards in education. Faculty members from many different departments use the library labs when they want to supplement instruction with computer usage. In addition, librarians teaching information literacy find the boards lend themselves well to demonstrating library resources online and can help promote group work. Elisabeth Knight at Western Kentucky University uses the electronic whiteboard for research instruction classes in the academic library. She finds the board especially valuable for demonstrating library databases and webpages.[36] After the initial training, she found the board relatively easy to use, although it takes some time to get used to the new method of presentation. Lessons can be created and saved for reuse, and images such as diagrams can be displayed and marked up during each class period and easily erased for the next class. Knight found the students were more interested in lessons with the use of the electronic whiteboard. At Portland State University (PSU), Robert Schroeder also found the use of electronic whiteboards in the library to have a positive influence on learning in the "affective domain."[37] The affective domain includes learners' motivation, attention, self-concept, and social interactions. Since this domain is much less quantifiable than cognitive learning, less research has been done in this area. With the use of electronic whiteboards in library instruction at PSU, it was found that students saw the library as a more active place where collaboration is encouraged. This perception helped to increase student engagement in library instruction sessions.

## Using Video for Teaching and Learning

According to a 2014 report by Google, more college-age students today view videos on YouTube than watch popular cable TV channels (see figure 4.2).[38] Google researchers also found that 98 percent of 18–34-year-olds watch videos on their smartphones compared with 81 percent who watch TV. Fifty-six percent watch videos on their computers, and only 19 percent use a tablet computer to watch videos. Increasing numbers of people of all ages also view videos on their smartphones.[39] In a case study by the Nielsen Company, video watching on the Internet by all people in the United States is growing, while TV watching is shrinking. A majority of video watchers now prefer to stream movies over the Internet rather than view them on cable TV. Statistics gathered by Nielsen show YouTube currently as the most popular digital video platform.[40] Clearly, online video is a medium that is very familiar for recreational viewing. Technological trends such as these are important for educators to pay attention to in order to reach students where they are most comfortable to better facilitate learning.

Learning with video resources has been studied for many years and has been shown to be an engaging and effective method of instruction. The use of video as an instruction tool began during World War II, when film clips were used for skills training. This led to the study of video in education and gave rise to the use of TV and films in K–12 education. With the creation of VHS and CD-ROM, video-based learning became even more common. The early days of video did not provide for much interaction since learners had to sit and passively watch the film all the way through, but the technology proved to be very engaging and motivating to students.[41] With the rise of the Internet and online video technologies, educators are able to control and customize video like never before. There are now many ways to create and use video in the classroom with free or inexpensive software. Sharing video tutorials is also simple and easy with cloud-based, social-networking applications such as YouTube. Commonly used software includes Jing, Screencast-O-Matic, Camtasia, iMovie, and saving PowerPoint slides with voice-over to video format. In addition, YouTube now has a recorder feature built in so that users can record from their computer and publish videos immediately. Most mobile devices such as smartphones and tablets will now record movies, which can be uploaded to social media and instantly published. While creating and sharing videos is becoming relatively easy and ubiquitous, it's important to follow good teaching practices when using video in the classroom for the best learning outcomes.

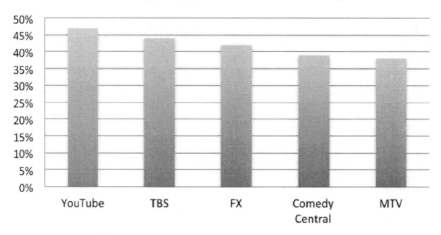

**Figure 4.2.   Percent of YouTube videos viewed by 18–34-year-olds versus cable TV (Nielsen, 2015)**

Studies have shown that video-based learning can increase learning outcomes when best practices are followed. Video has been shown to raise motivation by activating the emotional levels of students. Video can be particularly effective when used to show step-by-step learning procedures, especially when the information is presented in short videos that can be watched in sequence or when needed for specific learning objectives.[42] Video can also be a very effective learning tool when used to show real-life problems that students can discuss and use to develop problem-solving skills. It's important to remember that the best learning happens when learning is student centered. When learning with video, students should have control over the pace and content and learning should be self-directed with support from the teacher when needed. Some techniques for teaching with video include problem-based learning where short video clips are shown and students discuss the situation and do group problem solving; microteaching where small groups of students watch short video podcasts with teacher feedback on their performance in music or sports; video summarization, which involves extracting the most important points from a lecture and publishing a short summary video; and hybrid learning models such as the flipped classroom where an online video is assigned to students as homework and discussion of the material is held later in the classroom.[43]

In an article about teaching introductory geographic information system (GIS) software, the authors compared traditional text-based manuals with static screenshots with a redesigned online video manual that incorporated multimedia and interactivity.[44] They found that the redesigned materials improved information retention, reduced redundancy, and improved learning efficiency. Student motivation and interest in the materials also increased.[45] The multimedia materials provided an improved representation of the functioning of the GIS software and allowed students to download the materials to their mobile devices to view later in short video segments. The benefits of using this approach included more student control over learning since they could repeat sections of the material or skip over sections if not needed. Improved clarity of information through the use of multimedia resulted in students reporting increased confidence in using the GIS software.[46]

The flexibility of video instruction is of great benefit to student learners since they can review materials at their own pace and at a convenient time from multiple types of devices. Innovative tools are being developed to further increase the benefits of learning with video content, such as synchronized lecture notes showing both video and text, software for integrated discussion and commenting on video, indexing or tables of contents to allow jumping to different parts of a video recording, and video-annotation tools that allow students to reflect on performance or view instructor feedback. Another new advance is the availability of open educational resource (OER) repositories online where teachers can share materials such as video learning objects so that others can reuse and adapt the materials in their own class-rooms. Sharing of resources for library instruction programs is not as wide-spread as in other areas of education but has the potential to increase the effectiveness and quality of library instruction.

*Use of Video in Library Instruction*

In a recent article, librarians Alexandra Obradovich, Robin Canuel, and Ea-mon Duffy conducted a review of 140 U.S. and Canadian academic library websites to find out whether or not they hosted online video tutorials and if so, how they used them.[47] They were considering moving library instruction to the flipped classroom model, where videos are shown online before stu-dents meet with the librarian for in-class activities, and wanted to know the extent to which other academic libraries were using this model. With the flipped classroom model, class sessions are used to build upon the basic information presented ahead of time in videos, and more time is freed up for discussing important information literacy and scholarly communication top-ics in class. The researchers hoped the flipped classroom model would make library classroom sessions more interactive and student centered by using problem-based learning and group exercises to engage the students and pro-mote higher-order thinking.[48]

Of the 140 library websites reviewed, 107 provided online video tutorials. Some were located on a dedicated tutorial webpage, others hosted videos on YouTube, and a few embedded videos within subject or course guides. Of the library websites surveyed, only 2 percent included instructions on watch-ing the videos before library sessions, indicating that they use the flipped classroom model. The most common types of instructional videos found on library websites included catalog and database searching. Other types of videos found on about half of the library sites included instructions for using technology, how to evaluate sources, and using bibliographic management software. Less commonly found were videos on academic integrity and search strategies (see figure 4.3).[49] While videos are a popular and useful tool in library instruction, they must be updated often to avoid becoming outdated as interfaces and software changes. Some libraries avoid some of the work of updating custom videos by linking to vendor tutorials, especially for videos focusing on the use of software products.[50]

Another recent article compared new, open source software called Guide on the Side to traditional videos.[51] Guide on the Side embeds interactive tutorials, which display to the side of a webpage to guide students through using online library resources and materials. Guide on the Side tutorials are more interactive than video tutorials because they provide step-by-step in-structions while the students do hands-on learning on the webpage, working at their own pace. Images and quiz questions can also be added for additional

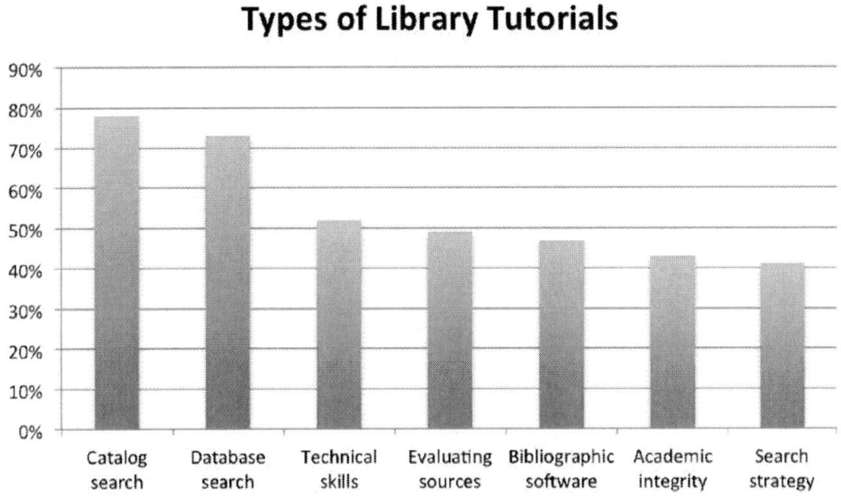

## Types of Library Tutorials

Figure 4.3. Types of library instructional videos (Obradovich, Canuel, & Duffy, 2015)

interactivity. Studies have shown that students prefer interactive videos compared with static videos when given the choice.[52] Interactive video has also been shown to increase retention of information. The study comparing the use of Guide on the Side to traditional instructional video found that creating Guide on the Side interactive tutorials actually took longer than creating traditional videos. The increased creation time was offset somewhat by the fact that Guide on the Side tutorials are easier to update.[53] For both types of tutorials, the longest and most important step is to create a script to follow based on the learning objects that will be taught. Guide on the Side may be a good option for those libraries wanting to replace in-person database demonstrations with online tutorials and for flipping the classroom. Traditional video tutorials may still be the best option for material not necessarily related to class assignments, especially if the videos are relatively short and divided up into specific topics.

While research has shown that multimedia resources increase learning and are engaging to students, some teachers still hesitate to incorporate video into their classes due to technical limitations and reluctance to spend class time setting up the technology. Also, some faculty may be worried about copyright infringement and may be unsure how to locate online resources that are appropriate and freely available for use in the classroom.[54] Online sources of multimedia are abundant, but it can be overwhelming to try to sort through them and find appropriate educational materials that are not restricted by copyright. At this time, a search for "library instruction" on You-

Tube brings up over 45,000 results. Fortunately, educators have created blogs and websites that help locate good materials. TeacherTube (www. teachertube.com) is one site that contains a wide variety of multimedia objects. TED Talks (www.ted.com) also contains hundreds of quality videos, including over 300 on library topics. A Media Specialist's Guide to the Internet website (http://mediaspecialistsguide.blogspot.com/) has many great resources and links to other sources of information for all types of librarians. The Media Education Lab at the University of Rhode Island (http:// mediaeducationlab.com/curriculum/materials) has links to many resources for teaching media literacy and includes video materials on copyright and fair use.

In an article about using multimedia in social science education, the author gives advice for college faculty wanting to incorporate multimedia into their class presentations in order to increase engagement and augment lecture presentations.[55] The author suggests adding short, humorous clips as an icebreaker activity at the beginning of a course. Taking clips from news sources may also be an option, especially in the social sciences. One great source for finding news clips is C-SPAN Classroom (www.c-spanclassroom.org/). Database vendors are also beginning to license packages of good-quality educational videos. For example, Kanopy Streaming Service and Alexander Street Press provide on-demand access to educational video materials. A good site for finding OER shared by educators is Merlot II (Multimedia Educational Resource for Learning and Online Teaching;www.merlot.org), which has thousands of reusable teaching materials, including multimedia. Over 300 results are returned when searching for "information literacy."

As with any technology, problems can arise that may discourage the use of video resources in the classroom. There are two basic methods of showing videos: streaming or downloading. Streaming is when the video is accessed directly from a web link or a database vendor's website. Streaming video can be accessed through a URL directly embedded in a presentation or course management system.[56] Problems can arise if the browser being used needs a plug-in to display the particular video format or if network speeds are not sufficient. The instructor has more control over a downloaded video, but copyright may not allow downloading for some resources. If downloading is allowed, this method may be preferred since access to web media may be lost if the resource is removed or replaced. Fair use usually allows for educational use of video through the course management system or in class, but the copyright restrictions should be checked for each resource used.

Even though many students today are very comfortable accessing and viewing video content on the web, some considerations need to be taken into account. First, if students will be required to link to a video outside of class, it is important to consider that not all students may have high-speed Internet access, especially to certain video formats. Be prepared to offer alternative formats and access methods. Also, when assigning controversial content that may possibly upset or offend some students, a content advisory message may need to be posted. Of course, all video content should be fully previewed before posting, and only content that meets specific learning objectives should be selected. Technical issues that can occur when using video in the classroom include video links that don't play automatically from Power-Point, loss of Internet connection, website inaccessibility, and browser in-compatibilities. In addition, when choosing video files, make sure that the image quality is appropriately high so that it doesn't appear pixelated when displayed on a large screen. Having good technology support is important, but it's also wise to have an alternative lesson plan in case things go awry.

## MULTIMEDIA CREATION BY STUDENTS

Besides teaching with multimedia learning objects, teachers can encourage students to directly create multimedia projects. Having students create their own learning objects will activate higher-order learning and help turn facts and lecture into fully integrated knowledge. Using technology is actually not essential to this kind of learning. In a 2014 study, the authors had students read about a concept from a textbook and then draw a representation of the concept.[57] This method of instruction was more effective in stimulating deeper learning than merely viewing multimedia objects.[58] Teachers can also use student drawings to evaluate learning. When reading from text-based materials alone, learners must construct their own mental model of the con-cept. Drawing a representation will help them discover what is missing from their mental model and help them generate a more in-depth familiarity with the concept. In order to draw a concept, students must select the most impor-tant information from reading a textbook and integrate prior learning in order to build an accurate mental model. Building on this concept, there is a new app for medical students called Draw It to Know It (https://drawittoknowit. com/) that implements this idea in mobile format.

In an article on promoting improved engagement with undergraduate sci-ence classes, the authors experimented with having students create their own podcasts explaining scientific topics.[59] While listening to podcasts can be described as use of multimedia, having the students actually create the pod-casts is much more interactive and requires much deeper learning than pas-sively listening to recorded lectures.[60] Students were engaged as knowledge creators rather than just passive receivers of information. They were required to use higher-order thinking skills such as analysis and synthesis in creating their own podcasts on a scientific topic. An interesting finding was that students who were otherwise not motivated in the class reported a higher level of interest when working on the podcasting assignment.[61] Multimedia projects such as this are of particular benefit to students who enjoy creative activities, and they are often the ones who are the least motivated in science education.

Henry Greene and Cheryl Crespi experimented with having groups of students create short videos for business school accounting and advertising classes.[62] The video assignment replaced a project presentation in the advertising class, and students were given the option of doing an extra-credit video in the accounting class. Students enjoyed the projects but were not given instruction on the use of video technology, so they reported some technical difficulties. The instructors found that students had much less experience with actually creating a video than they assumed. Students in the advertising class found the assignment to be more applicable to their future careers than those in the accounting class. The positive aspects of the assignments were increased student engagement, active involvement, group interactions, and enjoyment of the project.[63] Creating videos requires a lot of work by the students, but learning outcomes are increased due to the students having to fully know their assigned topic in order to synthesize the information, write a script, and record and edit the video to create a finished product worthy of sharing with the entire class. It may be more effective and less intimidating to make video creation an optional or nongraded activity. In library instruction, students could create videos on information literacy topics that could be shared with other students or published on the library YouTube channel.

## TEACHING WITH GAMING AND SIMULATION

Teaching and learning with gaming and simulation is a hot topic in education and becoming more accepted as research is released that shows the benefits of using game play and simulation for educational purposes. A "serious game" can be defined as one that is not created solely for entertainment but that has a serious purpose as well.[64] When using games for adult education, the main purpose of creating the game should be to meet specific learning objectives. Existing games, created for entertainment purposes, can sometimes be modified for a serious purpose. Games typically involve competition, which can be a powerful motivator for learners. An advantage of game playing in education is that the learner can be immersed in a role that simulates real-life experiences in a safe and experimental environment. Not all games need to be as realistic as a simulation in order to be effective. Relatively simple board games and quiz-based games have also been shown to be effective.[65] Well-designed games can serve to heighten a player's focus on a subject, thereby increasing learning outcomes. In order to draw the learner fully into the game, tasks should be presented that learners are capable of completing successfully. Games need to be designed for appropriate ages and should include a mechanism for presenting step-by-step instructions for successfully completing game tasks. Feedback on progress should be presented as the player progresses. Engaging games also present rewards for successful completion, whether it be winning or earning badges or access to new levels of game play. Creating learning outcomes during the design process should produce clear goals for the game. The creation of games often requires an interdisciplinary team of subject specialists, educators, and game developers.[66]

In an article on what teachers can learn from popular video games, the author reflects on the characteristics of commercially successful games that engage game players enough to motivate them to expend their time and continued effort in order to master a long and challenging video game.[67] Teachers strive, sometimes in vain, to get students to engage with educational subjects using traditional classroom techniques. Games, if well designed, have the power not only to engage students but to immerse them in the topic and hold their attention as they actively strive to master the game and its content. Well-designed games also give information on demand when the player needs help to be successful and to avoid too much frustration, which could lead to abandoning the game.

Popular video games have game-play manuals, maps, and instructions built in that can be accessed from a control panel when needed. Games challenge players to build up competence and then stretch to new and ever-growing levels of achievement, without being too hard to discourage players at the start. Well-designed games are customizable to player ability and learning styles. The best games allow players to create and build. For example, some games allow users to build their own maps or scenarios. Popular games allow players to practice their skills repeatedly to build up competence. Massively multiplayer online games (MMOG) also require players to collaborate and work together on mastering game levels. Each player brings unique skills and tools to game tasks, mirroring real-life cooperative skills that could translate to the workplace.[68]

In a 2011 article on the creation of a multimedia forensic science game, the authors explored the power of online games to increase interest and motivate students to pursue science careers.[69] The authors report on a game created from the popular television show *CSI* to teach forensic science skills. Middle school and high school science classrooms across the country were selected to participate in a study of the efficiency of the game in teaching content as well as creating positive attitudes toward science. Each class was assigned to one of three game scenarios that presented a crime scene and provided virtual training and tools to use when analyzing clues and collecting evidence. The goal of the game is to eventually present a solution to the CSI chief. Members of the American Academy of Forensic Science were consulted when creating the game to ensure that the science of the game was accurate.[70] Participants reported high levels of enjoyment and engagement with the game. When comparing pre- and post-tests administered as part of the study, a significant increase in knowledge was consistently reported across ages, cases, and locations in urban, suburban, and rural schools. Evidence was also found to indicate an increase in motivation for some of the students to pursue further studies in forensic sciences. The authors propose that games such as this one could be used with high school students as simulated apprenticeships or to explore careers that they may not typically be predisposed to exploring.[71] This strategy could also be effective in undergraduate settings.

## Using Gaming in Libraries

The use of gaming in libraries ranges from circulating board games and video games to fully immersive online games teaching library concepts. In between is the concept of *gamification*, which means using gamelike elements such as awarding badges in order to motivate, engage, and promote learning.[72] Activities that libraries have been using in the library for many years, such as scavenger hunts, can be successfully translated into computer games. Librarian game developers have produced successful library games with small budgets, but development can take a lot of staff time. Some tips for successful game creation include identifying the specific audience for a game, thoroughly testing every step of the game, getting feedback from potential game players, and balancing educational content and fun elements. Focus groups of potential game players are an essential resource for creating a good, fun gaming experience while successfully incorporating learning elements.[73] The time and expense of creating a game will need to be weighted against the appropriateness for the audience and the potential benefits in student engagement and learning outcomes.

## TEACHING WITH AUGMENTED REALITY AND VIRTUAL REALITY

Using augmented reality and virtual reality in education is a developing field related to games and simulation. Virtual reality (VR) uses technology to immerse a person in a simulated environment. Augmented reality (AR) is a variation of VR where the user sees objects superimposed upon the real world.[74] In an innovative project carried out in China, an AR game was created to teach library classification systems to elementary school students. Librarian staff members are limited in Chinese elementary schools, so it was hoped that AR would produce equivalent learning outcomes compared with in-person librarian instruction. In the library classification game, printed markers were created and placed around the library. Students scanned the markers and were given a corresponding game scenario depending on the location of the marker. Lifelike cartoon characters led the player through the game and provided spoken feedback. All students, regardless of gender and previously acquired game-playing skill, were able to complete the game successfully. Students enjoyed playing the game and were motivated to learn. In addition, the study pointed out that all students playing the game received the same instruction, compared to differing levels of instruction that can result from multiple librarians teaching with different methods and different levels of teaching skill.[75] Unfortunately, these technologies are relatively expensive, but some open source software for game creation is available. Teaming up with computer professionals may be a good idea for the creation of a complex online game.

## THE FUTURE OF MULTIMEDIA IN EDUCATION

Exciting new developments in VR are making this technology more accessible to educators. Google Glass was an early form of AR technology. This product combined a tiny screen and touchpad connected to glasses' frames using wireless technology to transmit photos or videos to a mobile device.[76] Online content could also be viewed, making it a possibility for use in AR applications. Another technology that is in the development process is Oculus Rift, which is a gaming headset for playing VR games. VR is also being used in journalism in order to immerse people in real-life stories. Nonny de la Pena is a journalist and researcher who has created several of these VR projects, which she calls "full-body journalism."[77] VR journalism allows participants to go places where usually only investigative reporters can go. VR allows participants to experience news stories in a very realistic way. Audio and video materials are of a very high quality, and users who don the headsets become emotionally caught up in the scenes unfolding before them. This technology is currently just as expensive as creating a full-fledged documentary film and requires teams of journalists, filmmakers, and computer technicians. In the future, with continued technological advances the library could be the place where community members come to experience immersive stories through VR and lifelike simulations.

## NOTES

1. L. Johnson, S. Adams Becker, V. Estrada, and A. Freeman, *NMC Horizon Report: 2015 Higher Education Edition* (Austin, TX: New Media Consortium, 2015), accessed September 30, 2015, http://cdn.nmc.org/media/2015-nmc-horizon-report-HE-EN.pdf.

2. Eunmo Sung and Richard E. Mayer, "When Graphics Improve Liking but Not Learning from Online Lessons," *Computers in Human Behavior* 28 (2012): 1618–25.

3. Richard E. Mayer and Gabriel Estrella, "Benefits of Emotional Design in Multimedia Instruction," *Learning and Instruction* 33 (2014): 12–18.

4. Ibid.

5. Steven J. Bell, "Stop IAKT Syndrome with Student Live Demos," *Reference Services Review* 35, no. 1 (2007): 98–108.

6. Ibid.

7. Judith Schweppe, Alexander Eitel, and Ralf Rummer, "The Multimedia Effect and Its Stability over Time," *Learning and Instruction* 38 (2015): 24–33.

8. Alexander Eitel, Katharina Scheiter, Anne Schuler, and Marcus Nystrom, "How a Picture Facilitates the Process of Learning from Text: Evidence for Scaffolding," *Learning and Instruction* 28 (2012): 48–63.

9. Michael V. Miller, "Integrating Online Multimedia into College Course and Classroom: With Application to the Social Sciences," *MERLOT Journal of Online Learning and Teaching* 5, no. 2 (June 2009): 395–423.

10. Bjorn H. K. Wolter, Mary A. Lundeberg, and Mark Bergland, "What Makes Sciences Relevant? Student Perceptions of Multimedia Case Learning in Ecology and Health," *Journal of STEM Education* 14, no. 1 (January–March 2013): 26–35.

11. Charles G. Prober and Salman Khan, "Medical Education Reimagined: A Call to Action." *Academic Medicine* 88, no. 10 (October 2013): 1407–10.

12. Nabil Issa, Mary Schuller, Susan Santacaterina, Michael Shapiro, Edward Wang, Richard E. Mayer, and Debra A. DaRosa, "Applying Multimedia Design Principles Enhances Learning in Medical Education," *Medical Education* 45 (2011): 818–26.

13. Ibid.

14. Richard E. Mayer, "Applying the Science of Learning to Medical Education," *Medical Education* 44 (2010): 543–49.

15. Richard E. Mayer, "Incorporating Motivation into Multimedia Learning," *Learning and Instruction* 29 (2014): 171–73.

16. Eunmo Sung and Richard E. Mayer, "Online Multimedia Learning with Mobile Devices and Desktop Computers: An Experimental Test of Clark's Methods-Not-Media Hypothesis," *Computers in Human Behavior* 29 (2013): 639–47.

17. Ibid.

18. Ibid.

19. Lori S. Mestre, "Matching Up Learning Styles with Learning Objects: What's Effective?" *Journal of Library Administration* 50 (2010): 808–29.

20. Ibid.

21. Ibid.

22. Alanna Ross and Christine Furno, "Active Learning in the Library Instruction Environment: An Exploratory Study," *Libraries and the Academy* 11, no. 4 (2011): 953–70.

23. Ibid.

24. Ibid.

25. Ibid.

26. R. Keith Sawyer, ed., *The Cambridge Handbook of the Learning Sciences* (Cambridge: Cambridge University Press, 2006), p. 9.

27. Ibid.

28. Bradford Lee Eden, *Enhancing Teaching and Learning in the 21st-Century Academic Library: Successful Innovations that Make a Difference* (Lanham, MD: Rowman and Littlefield, 2015).

29. Ibid.

30. M. A. Bell, "Why Use an Interactive Whiteboard? A Baker's Dozen Reasons!" *Teachers.net Gazette* 3, no. (1 (2002).

31. Heather J. Smith, Steve Higgins, Kate Wall, and Jen Miller. "Interactive whiteboards: boon or bandwagon? A critical review of the literature." Journal of Computer Assisted Learning 21, no. 2 (2005): 91–101.

32. Ibid.

33. William D. Beeland, "Student Engagement, Visual Learning and Technology: Can Interactive Whiteboards Help?" presented at the Annual Conference of the Association of Information Technology for Teaching Education, 2002.

34. G. Dantzker, "Student Perception of the Use and Educational Value of Technology at the STCC Star County Campus: Implications for Technology Planning," *Educational Resources Information Centre*, 2002.

35. Ibid.

36. E. Knight, "How Smart Is a Smart Board for an Academic Library? Using an Electronic Whiteboard for Research Instruction," *Kentucky Libraries* 67, no. 3 (2003): 4–7.

37. R. Schroeder, "Active Learning with Interactive Whiteboards: A Literature Review and a Case Study for College Freshman," *Communications in Information Literacy* 1, no. 2 (2007): 64–73.

38. Google, "YouTube Insights, Q2 2014," Think with Google, July 2014, accessed October 15, 2015, www.thinkwithgoogle.com/research-studies/youtube-insights-stats-data-trends-vol5. html.

39. Ibid.

40. Nielsen Company, "Case Study: The Evolution of Digital Video Viewership," Media and Entertainment, Nielsen Insights, September 25, 2015, accessed October 15, 2015, www. nielsen.com/us/en/insights/reports/2015/case-study-the-evolution-of-digital-video-viewership. html.

41. Ahmed Mohamed Fahmy Yousef, Mohamed Amine Chatti, and Ulrik Schroeder, "The State of Video-Based Learning: A Review and Future Perspectives," *International Journal on Advances in Life Sciences* 6, nos. 3–4 (2014): 122–35.

42. Ibid.

43. Ibid.

44. Nick Mount and Claire Chambers, "'I'd Rather Be Watching the Telly . . .': Do Rich Media Approaches Offer Real Teaching and Learning Benefits for GIS Software Tuition of Digital Natives?" *Geographical Information Science UK*, 2008: 285–90.

45. Ibid.

46. Ibid.

47. Alexandra Obradovich, Robin Canuel, and Eamon P. Duffy, "A Survey of Online Library Tutorials: Guiding Instructional Video Creation to Use in Flipped Classrooms," *Journal of Academic Librarianship* (2015), 751–757.

48. Ibid.

49. Ibid.

50. Ibid.

51. Susan Mikkelsen and Elizabeth McMunn-Tetangco, "Guide on the Side: Testing the Tool and the Tutorials," *Internet Reference Services Quarterly* 19, nos. 3–4 (2015): 271–82.

52. Ibid.

53. Ibid.

54. Miller, "Integrating Online Multimedia."

55. Ibid.

56. Ibid.

57. Annett Schmeck, Richard E. Mayer, Maria Opfermann, Vanessa Pfeiffer, and Detlev Leutner, "Drawing Pictures during Learning from Scientific Text: Testing the Generative Drawing Effect and the Prognostic Drawing Effect," *Contemporary Educational Psychology* 39 (2014): 275–86.

58. Ibid.

59. Mark Pegrum, Emma Bartle, and Nancy Longnecke, "Can Creative Podcasting Promote Deep Learning Content in an Undergraduate Science Unit?" *British Journal of Educational Technology* 46, no. 1 (2015): 142–52.

60. Ibid.

61. Ibid.

62. Henry Greene and Cheryl Crespi, "The Value of Student Created Videos in the College Classroom—an Exploratory Study in Marketing and Accounting," *International Journal of Arts and Sciences* 5, no. 1 (2012): 273–83.

63. Ibid.

64. D. Djouti, J. Álvarez, J. P. Jesel, and O. Rampnoux. "Origins of Serious Games. Serious Games and Edutainment Applications." (2011): 25–43.

65. Bohyun Kim, "Learning with Games in Medicine and Healthcare and the Potential Role of Libraries," In *Games in Libraries: Essays on Using Play to Connect and Instruct* (Jefferson, NC: McFarland, 2014), 152–170.

66. Ibid.

67. James Paul Gee, "What Video Games Have to Teach Us about Learning and Literacy," *ACM Computers in Entertainment* 1, no. 1 (2003): 1–3.

68. Ibid.

69. Leslie M. Miller, Ching-I Chang, Shu Wang, Margaret E. Beier, and Yvonne Klisch, "Learning and Motivational Impacts of a Multimedia Science Game," *Computers in Education* 57 (2011): 1425–33.

70. Ibid.

71. Ibid.

72. Carli Spina, "Gamification in Libraries," in *Games in Libraries: Essays on Using Play to Connect and Instruct* (Jefferson, NC: McFarland, 2014), 62–79.

73. Mary J. Snyder Broussard, "A Bag of Tricks for Successful Library Games," in *Games in Libraries: Essays on Using Play to Connect and Instruct* (Jefferson, NC: McFarland, 2014), 203–216.

74. Chih-Ming Chen and Yen-Nung Tsai, "Interactive Augmented Reality System for Enhancing Library Instruction in Elementary Schools," *Computers in Education* 59 (2012): 638–52.

75. Ibid.

76. Char Booth and Dani Brecher, "Ok, Library Implications and Opportunities for Google Glass," *College & Research Libraries News* 75, no. 5 (2014): 234–39.

77. Erin Polgreen, "Virtual Reality Is Journalism's Next Frontier," *Columbia Journalism Review*, November 19, 2014, accessed October 15, 2015, www.cjr.org/innovations/virtual_reality_journalism.php.

*Chapter Five*

# Mobilizing Teaching and Learning in Libraries

The use of mobile technology to enhance library resources and services in innovative ways is a growing trend in all types of libraries. Library users are already using mobile technology in their personal lives to find information, communicate with friends and family, shop, and keep track of daily appointments. Mobile technology allows people to look up information anytime, anywhere at the point of need, whether it is for work or personal life. In this way, mobile technology can be said to enable lifelong learning. Librarians have been experimenting with making library resources accessible on mobile devices in a variety of ways, as well as providing services through the use of mobile technology in the library. Many database vendors are now providing mobile apps or at least mobile-accessible websites. Access to library websites by mobile devices is growing, and demand for mobile library services will likely continue to rise. In order to keep up with demand and provide access to quality information resources in ways that library users have become accustomed to, librarians must consider increasing the mobilization of all library services and resources, including teaching and learning with mobile devices.

In a 2015 article on compulsory mobile education, the authors argue that mobile technology is so well established in everyday usage that it is already changing learning practices, so it is crucial that it be formally integrated into educational practices.[1] Educators need to learn new methods of teaching with mobile technology in order to use it effectively to enhance learning. Students need to learn to use mobile technology responsibly, as well as how to access scholarly information effectively with mobile technology. Mobile technology enables people to access information immediately while working, traveling, or researching, regardless of location or the time of day. In the past, when a need for information arose on the job, a computer workstation with access to the Internet would be needed to look up the information or check facts. If an Internet connection was not available, an information need might have gone unanswered or be forgotten. Mobile technology allows constant connection to the Internet with nearly ubiquitous access to information as long as a network connection can be found. For example, at our institution's medical center, medical residents are beginning to carry iPads with them as they do rounding in order to have access to point-of-care tools such as Dynamed and UptoDate. The ubiquity of mobile technology makes it a perfect tool for constant learning and accessible teaching.

Because mobile technology enables just-in-time access to information at the point of need, there has also been an increase in the acceptability of using mobile technology in the workplace for quick access to information. The accepted use of mobile technology in educational settings is also growing. Using mobile technology in real-world, case-based educational exercises is of particular use in reinforcing lifelong learning practices. Helping learners develop information searching and evaluation skills is crucial, with or without mobile technology. Librarians need to be well versed in the ways all our users access information in order to best serve our diverse populations. Increasingly, mobile technology can also help librarians move beyond the physical library to where our users work and study, as well as where community events happen, rather than waiting for users to come to us for services and resources. In the Google age, where searching is easy but not necessarily comprehensive or accurate, librarians need to reach out to users who may not know that better information is readily available through their library resources and teach them to effectively find and use that information.

## BACKGROUND AND DEFINITIONS

Mobile technology can be defined as the use of portable technology to enable access to the Internet from anywhere, anytime, using wireless technology. This definition includes smartphones and e-readers as well as tablet computers. Popular tablet computers include the iPad, Samsung Galaxy Tab (Android), Microsoft Surface, and Kindle Fire. While sales of mobile devices continue to rise exponentially, educational usage is still at the exploratory stage.[2] Many of the studies on the use of mobile technology in education report on the use of iPads in education since the iPad is currently the most popular tablet computer used in education.[3] Research on the effective use of mobile technology in education is developing slowly. In the research, learning with mobile technology is often referred to as *mobile learning* or *m-learning*. The study of m-learning is a new and growing field that seeks to bring about innovations in education through the use of mobile technology.

In a recent review article of the use of iPads in higher education, the authors found that students were motivated to use mobile technology, but faculty members were more skeptical of the educational effectiveness of the technology. While mobile technology seems to promote communication and collaboration, faculty worry about easy access to the Internet and social-networking apps distracting students from learning tasks.[4] There is still much work to be done in identifying sound pedagogical practices for using mobile technology in education, as well as establishing guidelines for teaching and learning with mobile technology.

## GROWTH OF MOBILE TECHNOLOGY

All over the world, mobile technology has become more affordable and wireless networks have become faster and more widely available, causing exponential growth in the use of mobile technology. According to the Pew Research Center, in 2015 90 percent of Americans owned a cell phone, while 42 percent owned a tablet computer and 32 percent owned an e-reader. Almost two-thirds of the U.S. population are smartphone users who are reported to go online frequently using their phones.[5] Smartphone usage around the world is also growing fast. According to the Pew survey, some smartphone users depend on their phones to access the Internet, especially young adults and those from lower-income brackets who do not have access to desktop or laptop computers. In the United States, it is estimated that one-third of all smartphone owners go online from their phones most of the time. They use their phones to look up information on a variety of topics whenever and wherever the information need arises (see figure 5.1).[6] According to the research, over 50 percent of smartphone owners use their phones to access health information and do online banking. Other common uses include job searching, house hunting, and accessing government services online. Around 30 percent are reported to use their smartphones to access educational content and online courses. Clearly, mobile technology is integrated into many people's daily lives and is often the first place they turn to find information when needed.

## USE OF MOBILE TECHNOLOGY

It is important for institutions and libraries to understand our patrons' use of technology, including mobile technology, in order to provide user-centered services and to effectively teach with mobile technology. While mobile technology usage is growing across all demographics, college-age adults are reportedly the biggest users of mobile technology. Most have smartphones and laptops, but many are also purchasing tablets and e-book readers.[7] A

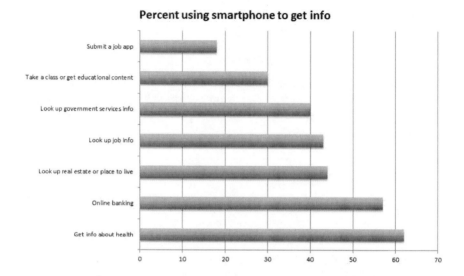

**Percent using smartphone to get info**

Figure 5.1.   More than half of smartphone owners have used their phone to get health information and do online banking (Pew Research Center, 2015)

growing number of these students are using their mobile devices for academic purposes (see figure 5.2). [8] Higher education institutions especially should pay attention to the growth in mobile technology when planning for future services and resources.

In a study of student mobile usage at the University of Central Florida (UCF), researchers found that student ownership of a tablet computer was academically beneficial. Over 80 percent of students who owned tablet computers used them for academic purposes such as looking up information and accessing e-books. While students are already using mobile devices for access to information, the UCF study determined that students are in need of support in effectively using mobile technology for learning. [9] There is a need to promote information literacy and critical thinking for deeper learning and to increase engagement with online learning tasks. There is also a need to help students select helpful academic apps from the wide range of apps available. Training for faculty members wanting to use mobile technology in meaningful ways in the classroom is also needed.

There are a wide variety of mobile apps available for teaching and learning. The top categories of apps used by mobile device owners include social networking, music, games, navigation, and general entertainment apps. [10] Many of the top apps used by students every day to find information can be used in the classroom to enable learning. This includes social-networking apps, which can be used for teaching collaboration and communication. Most

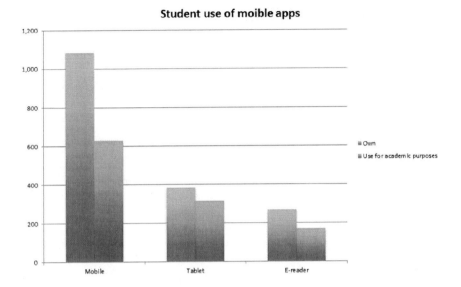

**Figure 5.2.    Use of mobile apps for academic purposes (Chen & Denoyelles, 2013)**

student use of mobile apps occurs outside of classrooms, with limited guidance from educators. Mobile technology is convenient, flexible, interactive, and engaging to students. Guidance in developing the digital literacy skills needed to effectively access, evaluate, and manage information accessed through mobile technology is critically needed, and librarians are uniquely positioned to provide this guidance. As a starting point, librarians can gather lists of high-quality apps available for their particular constituencies. In addition, providing mobile devices for patrons to use in the library as well as librarians personally becoming familiar with mobile device usage is a first step to providing the support needed for effective mobile learning in our institutions and within our communities.

In a recent study, researchers surveyed academic librarians nationwide about the implementation of mobile technologies at their institutions. Responses to the survey indicated that many librarians believed that the library should offer a wide variety of resources and services via mobile technology.[11] A majority of respondents indicated that the library staff has the responsibility for implementing mobile access to resources and services rather than hiring professionals from outside of the library. Most of the survey respondents indicated that they had implemented at least one mobile service or were planning to implement a mobile service at their library in the future. Types of services implemented included mobile access to lockers and study room reservations, mobile alerts for new services and resources, and the use of tablet computers by librarians for roving reference services. In the same study, the researchers found that students were already using mobile devices for academic work and were interested in mobile services to help integrate library resources into their learning practices. The most commonly requested services included access to the library catalog and access to online articles.[12] With the proliferation of mobile resources and services, some librarians are already teaching people to use these new tools on a daily basis.

Clearly, there is a need for increased mobile services for teaching and learning, but many libraries are either reluctant to spend limited budgets on new and expensive technology or lack the training and support necessary to implement these programs. Support for online learning and increasing technology innovation, including mobile access, is becoming available from a variety of sources seeking to enhance educational practices. For example, the State University of New York (SUNY) has initiated a program to support professional development of faculty members who would like to experiment with using cutting-edge technologies in their courses. The Tools of Engagement Project (TOEP) website includes training on the use of many different technologies that can be used in education, including mobile apps, social media, video, and other tools.[13] The goal of the project includes increasing student learning and engagement as well as helping teachers go beyond traditional teaching strategies to embed 21st-century skills in the curriculum.

## TEACHING AND LEARNING WITH MOBILE TECHNOLOGY

Some librarians are beginning to adopt mobile technology into their teaching practices in addition to continuing to develop other mobile library services. Mobile technology is especially useful in library teaching because it engages students and promotes student-centered learning.[14] Using mobile technology in the classroom also encourages social learning as recommended by good pedagogical practices. Student use of mobile technology enables personalization of the learning environment and control of learning pace as well as allowing for multiple learning styles, especially visual and kinesthetic styles. Mobile technology can also be used for real-world, authentic learning.[15] Mobile technology provides instant access to information whenever and wherever needed, allowing students to look up answers when questions arise. When students engage in this kind of learning in the classroom, librarian teachers can be available to guide them in improving the effectiveness of their search for information. Mobile technology also enables multimedia learning with easy access to videos and Internet content. The possibilities that mobile technology opens up for teaching and learning are exciting, but many more studies need to be done on the pedagogy behind teaching with mobile technology in order to use this technology effectively.

Every year, the *Horizon Report* identifies top challenges facing education today. Two of the top challenges discussed in the 2015 *Horizon Report*, informal learning and personalization, can be improved with the use of mobile technology.[16] Informal learning takes place in the real world and is characterized by self-directed exploration. New models of learning such as competency-based education emphasize informal learning. Traditional education is also beginning to recognize that the boundaries between formal and informal learning are fluid. Teachers can leverage the use of mobile technology to facilitate informal learning beyond the classroom. Personalization of learning is a growing focus of education that is difficult to implement with current technologies. Learning can be said to be more personalized when it allows for individual student-learning pace, interests, needs, and background. The use of mobile technology is a highly personalized experience, offering choice of setting, a multitude of personalizable apps, and access to personal contacts and social connections. Online learning environments offer some personalization features, but faculty members need training in order to fully implement personalized online learning. Online learning software needs to be developed further in order to provide better-quality, data-driven personalized environments for individual students but is already making content available through mobile-optimized interfaces or mobile apps such as the Canvas app. Mobile technology can be used to personalize a learning environment for online students to integrate schoolwork with social networks, calendar, e-mail, and other online activities. Some educational institutions are implementing tablet computer programs in order to personalize learning for their students in this way.

## A Framework for m-Learning

Many of the current studies of teaching and learning with mobile technology focus on the technology used, but in order to effectively use mobile technology in education, we need to start with a good understanding of the pedagogy behind mobile learning or m-learning. In a recent study of the pedagogy of teaching with mobile technology, the authors offer a useful framework for understanding mobile learning. The framework includes three main components uniquely provided by mobile technology that can be used to enable learning.[17] The three components include enabling collaboration, providing authenticity, and enabling personalization. Each of these components can be leveraged to positively affect learning outcomes. In addition, mobile technology enables flexible, social learning independent of space and time across all of the three components. Understanding all of these components of mobile technology will help guide the design of effective mobile learning activities. We will examine each of the three components in more detail below.

## Collaboration

The collaborative aspect of mobile technology comes from enabling conversations between the instructor and between students in a class. Students are enabled by mobile technology to connect to peers, the instructor, and other experts immediately through social networking and other mobile tools without the confines of time and location. Conversations can be spontaneous and personal. Mobile technology also enables data sharing between students and teachers.[18] For example, students can share work using cloud apps such as Google Docs or other available apps that allow online creation of shareable documents and multimedia content. Instructors can give feedback on assignments quickly and easily, and peer review of student work is also enabled through mobile platforms.

## Authenticity

The authenticity aspect of mobile technology comes from enabling real-world situations in learning. For example, mobile technology can enable students to learn while participating in actual tasks in the community or through realistic simulations accessed through mobile technology. Learning in the actual context of the subject of study, instead of in a classroom, can be described as authentic learning. Learning tasks that the students complete can be carried out in a real-world context using real-life practices. This authentic learning is very motivating to students and can increase engagement with the subject and positively affect learning outcomes.[19] An example of this kind of learning would be student use of tablet computers to access library resources for further information while at a museum or cultural event.

## Personalization

The personalization aspect of mobile technology comes from enabling self-regulated learning. For example, mobile technology allows students to set the pace of learning, enabling choice of content to study and opening up options for place and time of learning. Mobile technology can also allow students to set individualized goals through the use of a wide variety of educational apps. It also enables a highly customizable interface, which has been shown to increase learning outcomes. For example, students can personalize settings on mobile devices to optimize their learning environment. Some apps use the global positioning system (GPS) feature of mobile technology, which can also provide personalization when combined with educational apps that deal with a physical location. A "pervasive learning environment" can be set up for an individual learner with custom settings, links, and apps.[20] Increased learning comes from creating an optimum student learning environment, responsive to each individual's needs.

## SAMR Model for Evaluating Technology

The use of technology in education is not always effective in teaching and learning and should not be used without a good pedagogical purpose. Technology can be merely substituted for traditional learning methods, or it can be used to truly transform teaching and learning. Beyond substitution for traditional methods, the use of educational technology can be used to augment learning tasks, modify learning tasks, or completely redefine teaching and learning. The SAMR model can be used for evaluating the level of technology use in teaching and learning. The model guides teachers in asking questions about the use of technology in educational practices to determine whether the use of the technology will enable higher-order thinking skills and engage students in authentic learning tasks. The SAMR model provides a scale to measure the level of student engagement and innovation that technology affords for a specific teaching task.[21] Not every use of technology needs to be innovative. Different tasks may require different levels of technology integration.

SAMR stands for substitution, augmentation, modification, and redefinition:

*Substitution*

Is anything gained by using the technology? At this level, new technology is used as a substitute for a traditional learning task. For example, mobile technology can be used for traditional educational tasks of reading or note taking.

*Augmentation*

Does using the technology add new features that improve the learning task? At this level, technology enhances learning but doesn't change the task. For example, highlighting or annotating text with a mobile app improves the efficiency of the task but doesn't change it.

*Modification*

Does the use of technology significantly change the learning task? At this level, the task is actually changed by using technology. For example, using mobile technology to create a video presentation significantly modifies the learning process.

*Redefinition*

Does the technology enable a truly innovative task that would not have been possible without the use of the technology?[22] At this level, higher-order thinking skills are enabled and learning is extended beyond the traditional classroom. For example, mobile technology can be used to collaborate with other students around the world and open up new experiences and previously inaccessible learning opportunities.

Using the three-part framework for m-learning developed in the study mentioned above, educators can move teaching and learning with mobile technology toward the top level in the SAMR model, where technology redefines educational practices.[23] The following are some examples of innovative uses of mobile technology in education that redefine learning and include good pedagogical practices:

- Participation in a Twitter discussion during a presentation by a subject expert followed by in-class discussions
- Participation in an online game or simulation that involves role-playing in real-world situations in collaboration with other players
- Creating shared documents, graphs, charts, and drawings from participation in a group project situated within a community setting
- Creating a group video or online picture blog from a field trip activity
- Recording a video during a sports activity to analyze and improve performance

While studies have shown that students eagerly embrace mobile technology, faculty and librarians are often reluctant to implement mobile technology in their teaching practices. Using the SAMR model and the framework for m-learning given above may help inspire librarian teachers to experiment with some of the components that mobile technology uniquely provides and could help push teaching with mobile technology to the next level.

## USING MOBILE TECHNOLOGY IN LIBRARIES

Since so many people are now accessing resources through mobile devices, it is clear that libraries can better support the teaching and learning missions of their institutions by providing mobile access to library resources and services. Many libraries are finding creative ways to support mobile access and also offering new, innovative services using mobile technologies. Some of the ways in which libraries support mobile access include suggesting apps, promoting vendor apps for access to information resources, providing mobile-accessible websites, creating a mobile app for access to library services, loaning iPads to library users, providing reference service from iPads, and supporting tablet initiatives in our institutions and communities. We will examine each of these services in more detail with examples from different types of libraries.

## Suggesting and Evaluating Apps

There are apps available for every task, subject, and learning need. Sifting through the large numbers of apps for each situation and need can be overwhelming. Teachers need help finding and choosing appropriate educational apps. Students need help identifying apps for study and research. Apps can also be identified to introduce community members to important services and resources that they might otherwise not be aware of. Librarians can provide an important role in identifying and evaluating apps for the needs of their patrons. Many libraries now evaluate and suggest apps for their users on their websites. When evaluating apps, besides considering the task to be completed, it is important to consider the context in which the app will be used and evaluate the appropriateness for that context. Librarians should try out apps and evaluate the ease of use, identify any limitations to use, and check for bugs before recommending them. The value of the app as opposed to the cost is also an important consideration. [24] There are many very valuable free apps, but ads may be included, which may impact the user experience.

There are many online sources for evaluating educational apps. For example, *THE Journal* lists the top 10 iPad apps for special education, as well as their criteria used in identifying the top apps, in the June 2013 issue. [25] The apps listed range from an app for helping develop social skills to apps that enable translation of words into symbols for students who need an assistive word processor. There are also apps for video scheduling, increasing student motivation, and visually representing the concept of time. Most of the apps are available for under $20. Some great apps for teaching and learning in all settings include:

Apple productivity apps—create documents, spreadsheets, and presentations

Educreations—easy video-creation software

Evernote—take notes, save web clips and images, and sync between devices

Explain Everything—create interactive screencasts and animations

Good Reader—read, edit, annotate, and create new PDF files from mobile devices

Google apps—create and edit Google docs and access shared documents

iTunes U—create and access online courses from mobile devices

Kahoot—create mobile-accessible surveys and quizzes

Penultimate—write or sketch on mobile devices

Remind—automatically text reminders to students or parents

ShowMe—easily create and share video lessons
Skitch—create shared visual images to teach and learn

Many more apps for specific subjects and learning tasks can be found by searching the Internet or by browsing the Apple store and Google Play store.

## Mobile Apps for Libraries

Creating a mobile app for access to library services and the library catalog is becoming more important with the growth in personal usage of mobile technology. Making the library website mobile friendly is important, but the benefit of creating an app is that it can be customized to provide the most commonly used mobile services and is quickly accessible without a browser search. Using companies such as Boopsie, which develops mobile apps specifically for libraries, can simplify the process of creating a library mobile app. If technical library staff members with mobile technology expertise are available, in-house development of a mobile app may save money. Many public libraries have created mobile apps with access to look up and check out e-books online. Academic libraries may provide access to the library catalog and other services, such as study room checkout, through their mobile apps. An innovative app created by the New York Public Library called Biblion provides access to digital images, text, and multimedia relating to the 1939–1940 World's Fair.[26] The Biblion app allows users to browse through the app's contents in a variety of ways, which can be personalized depending on user preferences. The types of apps that can be created are limited only by user needs and librarian imagination.

## Tablet Loan Services

Another innovative service being explored in libraries is the loan of tablet computers to library users. Desktop computers have long been provided for patrons to access the Internet at most libraries. Laptop computers and tablet computers can also be provided for a mobile experience within the library. At Boise Public Library, the Main Library now provides kiosks with laptops and iPad computers for library card holders to check out and use anywhere inside the library.[27] Library patrons had been asking for portable computers for a long time according to library staff. In addition, tablet computers are easier for children to use than desktop computers, and they allow for easy collaboration and give users more flexibility to move around the library. Plans are underway to expand the program in the Boise Main Library as well as in other branch libraries. Mobile technology can be cheaper than purchasing traditional desktop computers, so new programs can be implemented with existing funds for upgrading computer technology by substituting tablet computers for desktops.

## Roving Reference Service

Tablet computers can enable librarians to move out from behind the information desk and out of their offices to where their users are working, studying, or living. Recent research has shown that many students are not using academic library resources. Other research shows that library users are reluctant to approach the information desk to ask questions.[28] One solution may be the use of tablet computers by librarians, which enable them to provide services at the point of need. This service has been around for a while now and is also called *roaming reference* or *offsite reference services*. Tablet computers are perfect for this task as they are light and portable but offer a larger screen than a smartphone, making them perfect for demonstrating the use of library resources and quickly looking up information. With the use of tablet computers, librarian teachers can provide instruction at any time or place when a teachable moment arises.

Areas outside the library where librarians could offer roving reference service include writing centers, computer labs, student residences, and other places such as cafeterias where potential library users congregate. In a 2014 case study, librarians initially felt awkward approaching students outside the library. Working in pairs helped to increase the librarians' confidence. An increased use of library services resulted from the case study, and student information-seeking behavior was shown to have improved after interactions with a librarian.[29] Although students may initially feel they are doing fine on their own, after interaction with a librarian they may realize the value of library resources to save them time and improve their research practices. Mobile reference services can also be successfully used in outreach to faculty and researchers, as well as clinical staff and other community members who do not have time to physically come to the library from their places of work.

## Mobile Devices in the Classroom

Initiatives to place mobile technology in the hands of students have been reported on in the literature for many years and range from assigning laptops, Chromebooks, or iPads to all students to using personal devices in the classroom. The latter type of program is referred to as *bring your own device*. Mobile devices are used in the classroom to look up information, access educational apps, or take online polls and assessments, as well as to enable participation in online activities and games. The Pew Research Center recently conducted a national survey of writing teachers and reported that 73 percent used mobile technology in their classrooms.[30] While the use of mobile technology in the classroom has been found to be engaging and motivating to students, few studies have demonstrated actual academic improvement from the use of mobile devices. Some of the mobile technology activities used by the writing teachers in the Pew survey included searching for online information, accessing and submitting assignments online, developing and sharing writing online, participating in online discussions, editing the student's own assignment as well as peer writing assignments, and enabling timely feedback from instructors for the improvement of writing skills. In addition, mobile technology can enable access to online textbooks. Online textbooks may be shared, open educational resources (OER) or created by the teacher through software such as Apple iBooks Author or library e-books. These materials are personalized to the course and may be much more up to date than a traditional textbook, which takes several years to publish and may be outdated by the time it is released for student use.

## Tablet Computers in Library Instruction

Tablet computers can also be used for more flexible and engaging library instruction sessions. In a 2014 article, the author reports on a project in an academic library where 25 iPads were purchased for hands-on library instruction sessions since a traditional computer lab was not available in the library. Previous to the iPad project, students were asked to bring their own laptops to library instruction sessions, which had mixed, often unsuccessful, results. The iPads are more mobile and less intrusive than laptops and allowed greater collaboration between students as well as ensuring that all students had access to hands-on practice.[31] The use of tablets in library instruction allows the librarian to move away from a traditional lecture model and allows students to experiment with solving their own research problems through trial and error and by collaboratively working with other students. The librarian guides the class session and keeps the students on task. While possibly taking more time than the traditional one-shot methods of instruction, teaching with mobile technology allows librarians the opportunity for increased interactions with individual students.

Putting mobile technology in the hands of all librarians is the first step to enabling teaching and learning with mobile technology in libraries. At the University of Washington Health Sciences Library, we began using tablet computers in 2011, and a successful pilot project soon led to purchasing tablets for all librarians.[32] We purchased both iPad and Android devices and trained librarians in their use. Librarians reported the tablets were helpful in completing their daily tasks as well as for use in outreach activities. Using mobile technology enabled librarians to do education while in clinical settings, at School of Medicine resident education meetings, when teaching evidence-based medicine, and when providing patient educational materials at outreach events. We also were able to try out and evaluate apps from library resource vendors as well as general educational apps in order to recommend them to our users. New librarians are given tablets in addition to a laptop or desktop computer, and tablets are upgraded regularly as funding allows.

## Tablet Computer Initiatives

An exciting new trend in education involves providing tablet computers for all students in a particular class, program, or school. Many smaller pilot programs have been done, but few institutions have implemented mobile technology for entire academic departments or schools.[33] Only a few large-scale implementations have been reported in the current literature. Large-scale projects require extensive financial and administrative investment, prior preparation, and extensive training of faculty and staff. Early adopters of tablet programs in education report encountering many problems that we can learn from going forward. Large-scale implementation of mobile technology in higher education is still in an emerging phase, and more research needs to be done on best practices for implementation and effective usage in teaching and learning.

In some cases, pilot tablet computer programs have led to abandonment of the full-scale adoption of this new technology.[34] In others, early problems reported in the research have been solved with advancing technology. Problems such as the limitations of touch typing without a keyboard and insufficient wireless infrastructure have improved greatly. Many options for attaching keyboards to tablets are now available. Problems with insufficient wireless infrastructure should be addressed before attempting the adoption of tablet initiatives, although upgrade costs may be prohibitive. Many public buildings and academic institutions are now fully equipped with adequate wireless access throughout most of the structure and sometimes even in outside areas. Lack of training for students and faculty is a problem that may also lead to failure of a mobile initiative. The support of technical services staff and providing online tutorials and guides on using the technology are crucial to success. Choosing apps for tablet computer initiatives can also be a challenge, and librarians can be of help with this important task.

Mobile technology should not be used in all situations and for all purposes. An important thing to consider when deciding whether or not to use mobile technology is considering if students will be distracted from learning by using the tablet to read e-mail and check Facebook instead of completing online research. Good instructional design will help minimize off-task behavior and keep students engaged. Tablets should only be used if they are integral to the learning activity so that students are engaged and don't have time for distractions. At other times, the tablets can be put away. Writing research papers or other activities that require a lot of typing are still best done on a laptop or desktop. Holding in-depth class discussions generated from a mobile activity is a good practice to use as a follow-up from mobile instruction. Using mobile technology in the classroom can increase student involvement with course content and lead to increased interactivity but may not be appropriate for all subjects or learning tasks.[35] The SAMR model and other frameworks for using technology can be used to determine appropriate and effective use of mobile technology for different situations and educational tasks.

## Student Perceptions

In a study of student opinions on the use of iPads in learning, students found the iPad relatively easy to use and intuitive to learn.[36] Students enjoyed using new technology in classes and appreciated experiencing new methods of learning with technology. Students also liked having easy access to look up information and do research in class, beyond using a textbook. Students often felt more involved with class discussions and group work. Some students felt it took too much time to figure out how to use the iPad for certain activities, and students were sometimes distracted by the apps on the tablet computers used in this study. Overall, students enjoyed the personalized nature of using mobile technology and the hands-on experience. Connectivity, limitations of apps, and touch typing were some drawbacks reported, but some of these limitations have been improved with updated versions of tablet hardware and software.

## Faculty Perceptions

Support for faculty teaching with technology is essential to the success of a tablet mobile learning initiative. Some faculty members need lots of training in using new technology effectively.[37] Faculty centers with expert staff for teaching support and faculty peer coaching can be very helpful. Repositories of apps to choose from are useful in narrowing down the wide variety of apps available for teaching and learning. When teaching with mobile technology, the instructor's role is more of a facilitator, and there is a need to adjust teaching methods to accommodate this new role. Some faculty members may initially be uncomfortable with this new style of teaching. However, faculty members who participate in mobile technology programs observe that students are more engaged and empowered when using mobile technology.[38] Mobile technology is also valuable for extending learning for those needing help and for accommodating alternative learning styles. Teachers also may need help adjusting assessment practices when using mobile technology. Trained support staff and instructional designers can be crucial to the success or failure of a mobile technology initiative. Since the library is a community space, training and support can be effectively offered from within the library. Librarians are often involved in helping train faculty as well as hosting technical support spaces for mobile technology programs.

## Best Practices

Best practices can be divided into two categories: guidelines for the successful implementation of mobile programs and best practices when using tablets for teaching and learning. Some best practices for implementing tablet computer programs can be obtained from a review of the literature. One key component is that the wireless infrastructure needs to be sufficient for wireless connection in all classrooms and study spaces. When planning for a mobile device initiative, it's also important to make sure that all participants will have access to the technology. Plan for loaner devices in case of breakage or financial hardship.[39] Individual ownership is optimum for the best use of mobile devices, but loaner programs have also been successful in library spaces. Tech support needs to be sufficient, and trained personnel should be hired. Teachers need to be trained in using the technology as "expert" users so they can help students or community members. Faculty members need to learn how to teach effectively with mobile devices, and training is essential for truly innovative uses of the technology. Creating websites and tutorials to help students get started with mobile technology is also a good idea. Implementing cloud applications such as Google apps in support of collaborative learning is important in preparation for a mobile learning initiative.[40] Buy-in is needed by all stakeholders—faculty, staff, students, administrators, and community members—in order for mobile initiatives to be successful.

Best practices for the use of tablet computers in education can also be obtained from reviewing the literature. Tying mobile activities to well-developed learning objectives is the most important practice. Designing specific activities for mobile use will go a long way toward reducing student distractions and promoting engagement in the activity.[41] Tying activities to problem-based learning and real-world examples is also a key strategy. Students who are new to using mobile devices should be trained in their usage before classes start. Online FAQs and technology support should be readily available. Keyboards and styluses should be provided if needed. Preloading apps for teaching and learning is helpful so that class time is not wasted on downloading and installation. Providing mobile access to textbooks and course readings and providing apps for annotation and highlighting can help make a mobile tablet initiative successful since students will appreciate having all course materials accessible from their portable device. Providing mobile access to a course management system is also important for educational institutions. Libraries need to ensure mobile access to research databases and library resources from all types of devices if their institutions are considering implementing mobile technology initiatives. All educators participating in a mobile technology initiative should be fully committed to spending the time to learn to use mobile devices effectively in teaching and learning before the program is fully implemented.[42]

*Barriers to Implementation*

There are some barriers for student access to technology that need to be considered when implementing mobile technology in education. Technology problems with access to the Internet and bandwidth need to be solved before considering m-learning programs. Limitations of mobile learning should be considered, and educators should make conscious choices about whether or not to use mobile technology for specific learning tasks. In order for the use of mobile technology to be truly innovative, the use must be transformative and not just a substitution for established methods of teaching. Support for students in information literacy, critical thinking, and collaborative learning while teaching and learning with mobile technology are very important considerations. Less mature students will need support in learning to use the technology appropriately.[43] Peer support for technology learning is often very successful, with the student-run help desk being the most common model in higher education. Many times, these types of services are offered by the library or by technology services working within the library location in order to easily reach all users.

Faculty support and training is also crucial. Faculty teaching support centers can be a good source of support for technology integration into classroom teaching practices. When implementing mobile technology programs, it is important to realize that e-texts may not be available for all subjects and interfaces. The publishing world lags way behind in providing open access to educational materials. OER sharing projects can help with this issue as well as reducing the costs of purchasing textbooks. There is also a great need for better, more flexible e-formats other than PDF.[44] Apple has created iBooks Author software for enabling educators to create their own interactive learning materials. When implementing a mobile technology initiative, it is best to start with a pilot program and consider the specific educational needs that the program will meet in order to be successful.

*Library Roles*

The library's role in mobile learning initiatives can take many different forms. In the research literature, the following possible future directions for library support of mobile technology have been described:[45]

- E-textbook licensing and management for mobile access
- Teaching digital and information literacy with tablet computers
- Technical support for faculty and student devices
- Creation of videos and tutorials to support training and technology use
- Mobile website design for access to research materials and resources
- Creation of lists of mobile apps for teaching and learning
- Loaning of tablet computers for use within the library

Libraries may be involved in one or all of these forms of support for tablet computer initiatives. The important thing is that librarians are involved as partners with faculty, students, administrators, and community members in order to support the success of mobile technology initiatives. Getting the library involved in the early planning stages can be crucial to the success of the program.

## The Mobile Campus

Some elementary and secondary schools as well as a few higher educational institutions are going mobile in a big way and implementing mobile technology for all students and faculty. For example, at the University of Central Florida (UCF) faculty and students have campus-wide access to all educational software from any device. Central servers contain licenses for software products, and using Citrix virtualization, faculty and students can log in through campus apps or a web browser to access software as well as their personal files and the course management system from any device. Buy-in across campus was needed to implement such a large project, and significant funding was also crucial. The campus environment was also redesigned to enable mobile technology. Large computer labs were replaced with collaborative learning spaces.[46] Librarians in the health sciences support the UCF mobile campus with technology support centers and mobile-optimized learning spaces. They also provide online guides to the mobile apps used for research and study, which are loaded on all student tablet computers.

At Stony Brook University, health sciences librarians have been involved in the early stages of planning for a mobile technology initiative that will eventually provide iPads for all health sciences students. Librarians were involved in identifying e-textbooks and useful apps as well as completing training with other faculty champions in the best uses of the technology in order to train other faculty members. An emphasis was placed on exploring innovative ways to use the technology in the classroom rather than merely providing access to online materials. Apple education training was provided, and initial faculty trainees were given access to iPads for the training sessions and to work on creating their own educational materials. Training included learning the basic use of iPads as well as the use of Apple software such as Pages and iMovie. Faculty champions also explored the use of iBooks Author to create interactive learning modules and iTunes University, which is an online learning platform. Many apps are available for teaching and learning, and librarians can help identify the best ones for specific learning tasks and subjects. Apps that enable students to create their own learning products are especially important, as learning outcomes can be enhanced when students use advanced-thinking processes to complete projects that synthesize learning into a product such as a presentation or video.

# THE FUTURE OF MOBILE TECHNOLOGY IN
# TEACHING AND LEARNING

Mobile technology use will continue to grow. Students and community members will continue to demand more engaging instruction as well as anywhere, anytime learning. More research on the pedagogy of mobile learning is needed to inform best practices for teaching and learning with mobile technology. Reports on successful implementations are also needed as tablet computer initiatives grow in number. Studies on innovative and pedagogically sound uses of mobile technology are crucial for successful implementations. Librarians can support teaching and learning in all types of libraries through the integration of mobile technologies in their services and by providing access to mobile resources for all types of users. Partnering with our institutions and communities, librarians can help to increase access to resources and services through the use of mobile technology and help to bring about new and exciting innovations in teaching and learning. The library, acting as the core of the community, can be crucial to the success of mobile technology programs and initiatives that impact our institutions and communities to bring about innovations in teaching and learning practices. Using mobile technology, libraries can better provide resources and services for the lifelong learning needs of all library users beyond limitations of space and time.

## NOTES

1. Viktoria Joynes and Richard Fuller, "Legitimisation, Personalisation and Maturation: Using the Experiences of a Compulsory Mobile Curriculum to Reconceptualise Mobile Learning," *Medical Teacher* (2015): 1–7.

2. Lemai Nguyen, Siew Mee Barton, and Linh Thuy Nguyen, "iPads in Higher Education—Hype and Hope," *British Journal of Educational Technology* 46, no. 1 (2015): 190–203.

3. Ibid.

4. Ibid.

5. Pew Research Center, "Mobile Technology Fact Sheet," Pew Research Center Internet Science Tech RSS, December 27, 2013, accessed November 1, 2015, www.pewinternet.org/fact-sheets/mobile-technology-fact-sheet/.

6. Pew Research Center, "U.S. Smartphone Use in 2015," Pew Research Center Internet Science Tech RSS, April 1, 2015, accessed December 21, 2015, www.pewinternet.org/2015/04/01/us-smartphone-use-in-2015/.

7. Baiyun Chen and Aimee Denoyelles, "Exploring Students' Mobile Learning Practices in Higher Education," *Educause Review*, accessed November 1, 2015, www.educause.edu/ero/article/exploring-students-mobile-learning-practices-higher-education.

8. Ibid.

9. Ibid.

10. Ibid.

11. Angela L. Dresselhaus and Flora Shrode, "Mobile Technologies and Academics: Do Students Use Mobile Technologies in Their Academic Lives and Are Librarians Ready to Meet This Challenge?" *Information Technology and Libraries* 31 (2012): 82.

12. Ibid.

13. State University of New York, "Tools of Engagement Project (TOEP)," accessed December 14, 2015, http://sites.google.com/site/sunytoep/about.

14. Rebecca Sullivan, "The iPad in Library Instruction: Collaborative Inquiry for Information Retrieval," *College & Undergraduate Libraries* 21, no. 2 (2014): 232–38.

15. Ibid.

16. L. Johnson, S. Adams Becker, V. Estrada, and A. Freeman, *NMC Horizon Report: 2015 Higher Education Edition* (Austin, TX: New Media Consortium, 2015), accessed September 30, 2015, http://cdn.nmc.org/media/2015-nmc-horizon-report-HE-EN.pdf.

17. Matthew Kearney, Sandra Schuck, Kevin Burden, and Peter Aubusson, "Viewing Mobile Learning from a Pedagogical Perspective," *Research in Learning Technology* 20 (2012), http://www.researchinlearningtechnology.net/index.php/rlt/article/view/14406.

18. Ibid.

19. Ibid.

20. Ibid.

21. P. Brown, "A Guide for Bringing the SAMR Model to iPads," *EdSurge*, accessed October 15, 2015, www.edsurge.com/n/2015-02-06-1-guide-for-bringing-the-samr-model-to-ipads.

22. Ibid.

23. Kearney et al., "Viewing Mobile Learning from a Pedagogical Perspective."

24. Chen and Denoyelles, "Exploring Students' Mobile Learning Practices."

25. Randall Palmer, "The Top 10 iPad Apps for Special Education: Empowering Independence in SPED Learners: There's an App for That!" *THE Journal: Technological Horizons in Education* 40, no. 6 (2013): 10.

26. Lizzy A. Walker, "New York Public Library's Biblion App: A Review," *Idaho Librarian* 62, no. 1 (2012).

27. T. Vitu, "Boise Main Library Offers Laptops, iPads for In-House Checkout," *Idaho Business Review*, November 16, 2015, accessed November 20, 2015, http://idahobusinessreview.com/2015/11/16/boise-main-library-offers-laptops-ipads-for-in-house-checkout/.

28. Alison Sharman, "Roving Librarian: The Suitability of Tablets in Providing Personalized Help outside of the Traditional Library," *New Review of Academic Librarianship* 20, no. 2 (2014): 185–203.

29. Ibid.

30. Pew Research Center, "The Impact of Digital Tools on Student Writing and How Writing Is Taught in Schools," July 16, 2013, accessed December 21, 2015, www.pewinternet.org/2013/07/16/the-impact-of-digital-tools-on-student-writing-and-how-writing-is-taught-in-schools/.

31. Sullivan, "The iPad in Library Instruction."

32. Angela Lee and Ann Whitney Gleason, "Tablet Mania: Exploring the Use of Tablet Computers in an Academic Health Sciences Library," *Journal of Hospital Librarianship* 12, no. 3 (2012): 281–87.

33. Nguyen, Barton, and Nguyen, "iPads in Higher Education."

34. Colin F. Mang and Leslie J. Wardley, "Effective Adoption of Tablets in Post-secondary Education: Recommendations Based on a Trial of iPads in University Classes," *Journal of Information Technology Education* 11, no. 1 (2012): 301–17.

35. Ibid.

36. Jonathan P. Rossing, Willie M. Miller, Amanda K. Cecil, and Suzan E. Stamper, "iLearning: The Future of Higher Education? Student Perceptions on Learning with Mobile Tablets," *Journal of the Scholarship of Teaching and Learning* 12, no. 2 (2012): 1–26.

37. Jace Hargis, Cathy Cavanaugh, Tayeb Kamali, and Melissa Soto, "A Federal Higher Education iPad Mobile Learning Initiative: Triangulation of Data to Determine Early Effectiveness," *Innovative Higher Education* 39, no. 1 (2014): 45–57.

38. Ibid.

39. Rossing et al., "iLearning."

40. Mang and Wardley, "Effective Adoption of Tablets."

41. Ibid.

42. Rossing et al., "iLearning."

43. Mang and Wardley, "Effective Adoption of Tablets."

44. Hargis et al., "A Federal Higher Education iPad Mobile Learning Initiative."

45. Chen and Denoyelles, "Exploring Students' Mobile Learning Practices in Higher Education."

46. Toni Fuhrman, "7 Best Practices for Creating a Completely Mobile Campus," CampusTechnology.com, February 10, 2015, accessed December 21, 2015, https://campustechnology.com/articles/2015/02/10/7-best-practices-for-creating-a-completely-mobile-campus.aspx.

*Part III*

# Facilitating Learning in Library Spaces

*Chapter Six*

# Teaching and Learning in Library Spaces

Teaching and learning happens every day in library spaces, whether in support of lifelong learning in our communities or as part of the formal teaching and learning conducted in academic institutions and schools. Libraries are located in the center of our communities and learning institutions, and they can be said to be the center of teaching and learning for those communities. Academic libraries are an extension of the classroom, and public libraries are the source of freely available information for the entire community. The library building and the spaces within it can enable teaching and learning to a greater or lesser degree depending on the space design. In the past, libraries were designed around service points and storage of books and other materials. Today, libraries are reducing physical collections and service points and increasingly providing open, flexible, technology-rich spaces that promote learning and provide access to rich information resources in many formats. Activities conducted in the libraries of today are a rich mix of collaboration, socialization, information discovery, and creativity. Good library design supports these activities and focuses on the needs of the specific community of users served.

Libraries of the 21st century contain a wide variety of spaces from computer labs, PCs, and printers to group and individual study spaces and collaboration areas to spaces for social interaction. In addition, they might also provide places to eat and drink and, increasingly, places to access other academic or community services. Librarians can be instigators of change in a school's or institution's curriculum and support innovation by providing support for teaching and learning through innovative services, technologies, and spaces.[1] With the continuing trend toward increasingly electronic resources, print volumes are moving to storage, and library spaces are opening up for technology, collaboration spaces, and other services to support student success. Library classrooms are being remodeled to facilitate problem-based learning and group study, which also supports the flipped classroom model. Besides providing classrooms for teaching information literacy and database searching, library spaces can also support creating and sharing information with multimedia equipment and software, presentation studios, visualization tools, and access to other creative technologies that may not be available elsewhere on campus or are too expensive for individual academic departments to purchase on their own. Interdisciplinary learning can also be facilitated in the library since the library is a centralized space open to everyone in the community.

Library space is different than other community and academic spaces such as dorms, the student union, cafés, and other recreational areas. The library is not a living space or recreational space, rather it exists specifically to promote learning. Libraries are unique in our society because they

- focus on academic work and learning/knowledge seeking,
- are free and open to all members of the community, and
- provide services supporting academics and learning, as well as hosting other services needed by the community.

Living spaces are not as conducive to learning as library spaces, and the library's combination of technology and services make it the best location for a supportive learning environment. Because of the unique mission and place in the community that libraries hold, our buildings and interior spaces need to be carefully designed to fit the teaching and learning needs of all library users. They must also be flexible in order to change with changing community needs, requiring librarians to maintain an environment of constant assessment in order to remain relevant and vital to the community.

## The Function of Library Spaces in Education

The library space is an extension of the classroom and part of the educational experience. The library also supports faculty, the institution, and community initiatives. Students today expect a practical education, which includes learning transferable skills such as project management, communication, and teamwork. Collaboration is required on many course assignments and is a skill highly valued by employers. Library spaces provide areas in which students can practice collaboration and teamwork. Technology is needed to complete most assignments and access course materials. Libraries support all of these academic requirements outside of the formal classroom. With the rise of online resources, predictions of the obsolescence of the library proliferated but were proven wrong as librarians began converting book stacks to collaborative study and technology areas. This in turn has reenergized the library as a center of teaching and learning in academic institutions as well as in communities.[2]

Our library spaces support student learning and partner with educational institutions and communities to support their missions. In order to remain relevant in today's world, libraries and library missions can no longer be library centric. The library is a learning enterprise that may contain points of access for multiple collaborative services. In the past, library spaces have been designed around service points and service providers. Today, service points are being reduced and space is opening up for flexible, active teaching and learning. New and innovative spaces for teaching and learning are now being designed to foster higher-order thinking and learning on our campuses and in our communities. In an article on learning behavior and learning spaces, the author introduces the concept of *intentional learning*, which is defined as intentionally working toward the goal of learning.[3] Intentional learning is done outside of the classroom and involves students taking responsibility for their own learning. It can be said that most learning happens outside of the classroom when students study materials and information to construct knowledge. Students complete activities to further their own learning, practice higher-order thinking skills, set goals that are meaningful, and assess their progress and success in reaching their learning goals—all outside of the classroom. Much of this kind of self-directed learning happens in nonclassroom spaces such as the library.

In a study of students and faculty members and their use of study space for specific study behaviors, researchers found little agreement between students and faculty and between different institutions on the most important learning behaviors that study spaces should foster.[4] The only two behaviors that most faculty and students agreed on were the importance of providing spaces for studying alone and providing spaces for collaborative study. Of all the nonclassroom spaces available in higher education institutions where students can learn and study, libraries were overwhelmingly viewed by both students and faculty as the best spaces for fostering desired learning behaviors. Students valued library study spaces more highly than faculty for the most part, and faculty valued fostering other learning behaviors besides studying alone and collaborative study. Faculty valued discussing materials with other students much more highly than students valued this behavior. Faculty also valued students having discussions with others with different values, experiences, and backgrounds. The researchers found that the institutions studied did not have any study spaces that supported these types of behaviors well, except for in the library to some extent. While it can be said that an entire campus serves as a learning environment, few spaces beyond the library were viewed as fostering real learning behavior.[5] A stronger emphasis on fostering important learning behaviors, whether in libraries or in other study spaces, needs to be considered when designing and redesigning campus study areas.

When libraries are created as mere service points, students are seen as consumers of services and not as learners. In order to be true partners in education on our campuses, libraries need to be consciously designed to foster the learning behaviors that are valued by the learning community. A deep collaboration among faculty, students, librarians, and other educators and service providers needs to be created with the goal of student success in mind. Conscious thought about desired learning goals, relationships to be fostered, and the messages that our learning spaces send to students and faculty needs to be encouraged before embarking on design projects.[6] If librarians desire to have more impact on students and student learning, they must move beyond the traditional service-oriented model to become true collaborators in learning. The best library spaces are created as collaborative spaces supporting active teaching and learning as well as quiet study and reflection.

## THE EDUCATIONAL VALUE OF LIBRARY SPACES

The library spaces of today also support faculty teaching goals and research goals. Access to information is provided in multiple formats and may be almost completely virtual in some libraries. Faculty teaching centers, computer teaching rooms, and active learning labs are being created in libraries as partnerships to improve teaching and support innovation. Training and support for teachers is also sometimes offered in these new library spaces. Training for researchers on using specialized databases, evidence-based practice, and bioinformatics is being offered. Partnerships with academic departments support the teaching role of faculty, which has changed over time to be much more interactive and less didactic. Learning is no longer thought of as a response to instruction but as a holistic social process that is a result of providing opportunities to quietly reflect or discuss ideas socially.[7] Library spaces enable learners to find information but also to create knowledge and then share it with others.

Library spaces can extend to virtual spaces such as websites and course management systems. In a study of student reading practices, it was found that less than 30 percent of students in the study were actually aware of or used their course reading lists. After the course reading lists were embedded in the course management system with the help of library staff who supplied links to full text e-journals, websites, and scanned resources, almost half of the students were using the reading lists linked from the course management system.[8] This is one example of the ways in which libraries and librarians can support teaching and learning through virtual collaborations with academic faculty and administrators. By reaching out to departments, finding out their needs, and filling gaps in services, libraries and librarians can make a positive difference in supporting the educational mission of their institutions.

Well-designed library spaces are created intentionally in order to support the institution or community goals and mission. In a paper on designing next-generation learning spaces, researchers at the University of Queensland found that higher education leaders recognized that the learning environment can have a significant impact on learning outcomes and also positively impacts the student experience at the university. Well-designed, attractive learning spaces can also be a major factor in recruiting students as well as increasing retention.[9] Health sciences libraries are often one of the important stops for prospective medical students when they are touring medical schools. Considering the amount of time medical students spend studying, having an attractive and functional study space that supports multiple learning styles with support services conveniently located nearby can be a very positive factor for student success. Modern, well-appointed libraries can therefore be an incentive that draws students to an institution of higher learning and also helps retain them throughout their studies to graduation.

One concrete way that libraries support academic missions and goals is by providing study spaces that promote reading, research, reflecting, analyzing, and assessment. The time and effort students put into their studies outside of the classroom in order to create knowledge often determines their success or failure. Time spent on studying and preparing for class has a positive relationship to learning success and engagement with learning. Unfortunately, it is reported that more than 44 percent of students spend 10 or less hours a week studying for class, while faculty recommend that full-time students spend 25 or more hours per week studying.[10] Well-designed library spaces can help support student study habits and promote academic success as well as provide the services and technology needed for study and research.

In a study on student preferences for study space at Indiana University–Purdue University Indianapolis (IUPUI), the researcher found that the library was the preferred place for academic study over all other gathering places and seating areas provided by the university. The most popular place for study was the group study room, followed by group areas with comfortable seating. The traditional carrel was still found to be popular with some students, although carrels without nearby wiring for plugging in laptops were not used very often. Study spaces near natural light were also popular. The end-of-semester period saw a large influx of students, showing the need for increased capacity over normal day-to-day usage in order to accommodate peak study times.[11] This study points out the importance of considering all campus study spaces and fitting the library into the needs of the particular environment, as well as allowing for increased capacity at different times of the academic year when designing library spaces.

Many accrediting agencies have guidelines and specifications for supporting teaching and learning by providing adequate study spaces. Working with academic departments in aligning library study spaces with the requirements of accreditation bodies such as the Liaison Committee on Medical Education (LCME), Commission on Collegiate Nursing Education (CCNE), International Assembly for Collegiate Business Education (IACBE), and others is a very important task of academic libraries. Library spaces may need to change as accreditation requirements change, and librarians must work with departments and serve on accreditation committees in order to address space needs. Many accreditation bodies have study space recommendations, and the library should be a full partner with academic departments in ensuring they are providing adequate spaces for student study needs, not just in the years leading up to an accreditation visit but continuously. The library should be proactive in keeping up with current accreditation requirements and changes in the requirements in order to continue to support institutional goals and missions and provide the highest-quality services in support of student learning and teaching excellence.

Library spaces can also add value by being designed to support the specific needs of a particular section of library user groups. For example, the space needs of children, young adults, college students, adult learners, and the elderly all differ in many ways, and spaces need to be designed with the unique needs of each of these user groups in mind. In an article on a study of young adult spaces in public libraries, the authors report on an innovative method of assessing the use of library spaces. Librarians in libraries with specialized young adult areas were given video cameras and asked to give video "tours" of the library spaces. In each of the libraries studied, a young adult library user was also recruited to give a tour.[12] When designing library spaces, it's important to consider what types of activities will happen in the spaces, not just what furniture, equipment, resources, and services should be in the space. Studying the librarian and young adult videos explaining the usage of their library spaces allowed themes for activities and uses of the space to emerge. The teens typically focused on the activities done in the spaces, while librarians focused more on what services and resources the library space contains.

Although librarians and teens did not agree on the relative importance of all of the design elements found to be important to good young adult library spaces, several common themes emerged. Both librarians and teens highly ranked the importance of physical comfort, including comfortable furniture, natural lighting, windows and glass partitions, and casual seating with visual appeal. Important activities and information needs included access to leisure reading and computers for accessing the Internet, group spaces for socialization and hanging out, gaming spaces, and teen programs, as well as vending machines or cafés located nearby. Spaces designed especially for teens were also valued for quiet study spaces, access to computers and media for completing schoolwork, and to a lesser extent, academic study resource materials and reference services. Teens wanted a feeling of space ownership and valued a unique location in the library, separate from adult and child spaces. They also appreciated having input into the design and furnishings when renovations were being done. The study also found that having clear policies for space usage and marketing the spaces to the community were important considerations. Almost half of the librarians and teens in the study specifically expressed the importance of the young adult spaces in public libraries for academic study. Groups used the space for tutoring, group projects, and club meetings, as well as individual study. Some teens also expressed the importance of having a community study space away from the distractions of their home environment.[13]

Library spaces should support the mission of the institutions or communities in which they exist.[14] Learning spaces for each individual library should reflect the learning priorities of the institution, school, or community supported. Affiliated programs, initiatives, and other stakeholders will also be reflected in the design of library spaces. The members of the library community will determine the kinds of learning support needed, so assessment and involvement of stakeholders during the planning process or redesign process will make the library more useful to all constituents. For example, different spaces are needed to provide for both digital natives and digital immigrants, as well as for people who may not be familiar with using technology at all. Even while resources and media formats are changing rapidly, learner backgrounds are also changing. The younger generation may be more familiar with technology and various media, but they may also be in need of guidance and instruction in effective and efficient use of online materials. The older generation may need help accessing e-resources and using technology efficiently. Returning students, trying to keep up with more technologically savvy students, may need help getting up to speed in accessing resources and using new technology. These services may not be provided in the classroom, so many times the library is the place people go for help.[15] The library is a reliable, safe place that returning students can turn to for instruction on using technology to do research and in using software such as information management tools that instructors may assume students already know about.

When planning academic library spaces, there should be a strong vision for the future. Library spaces last for a long time and must continue to provide for the changing needs of the community for many years before money becomes available for a remodel or a new building. Comprehensive information on user needs should be gathered before design of the actual building begins. Assessment of library programs and services should also be done, and choices should be made about which services can be supported and which programs are essential for the unique community being served. Planning, therefore, should be collaborative and include all stakeholders. Interactive-space design workshops can be very successful, especially when held in the space to be designed or redesigned.[16] Community members or specific user groups can be invited into the library space and asked to participate in planning activities. This not only helps in the design of library spaces but creates buy-in and ownership of the process among stakeholders. Space is a precious resource on today's campuses, so libraries need to be designed collaboratively and with a clear idea of the value they will add to the institutional vision and mission.

## THE PEDAGOGY OF LIBRARY SPACES

Learning spaces should align with social pedagogy and support collaborative learning as well as supporting quiet study. Experience with team-based learning projects is valued by employers as a skill needed in professions today. The focus is shifting from designing spaces for teaching to creating spaces where learning happens and knowledge is created. These spaces need to serve multiple learning styles and should include quiet spaces for reflections, social spaces for discussion, and group study areas for collaborative project work. Learning processes require quiet reflection, learning through conversation with others, and learning by doing. Well-designed library spaces need to provide for all of these learning processes in order to serve all of their constituents' needs. In addition, well-designed libraries contain spaces for active learning and self-directed learning. Constructivist learning models ask us to move away from lecture toward more active learning. Library spaces can continue learning outside of the classroom by providing for all kinds of study, whether it be quiet reading, collaborative study in groups, or use of technology, and in many libraries learning can continue 24 hours a day. The new model of teaching by flipping the classroom, which requires students to watch lectures and do exercises outside of class in order to prepare for classroom discussions, should be supported by providing library spaces to access videos, online resources, and other materials required for the assigned classroom activities. Providing these kinds of spaces makes the library a true partner in teaching and learning.

In order to promote deeper learning, time is needed outside the classroom for learners to reflect on their learning, to fully understand the material presented in class, and to integrate the material with previous learning and life experiences. Library spaces can provide areas conducive to reflective study where students can also receive support for learning through services such as writing centers, tutoring services, and technology to access information and online resources. Information literacy instruction, which often takes place inside library technology spaces, also supports deeper learning by teaching critical-thinking skills and higher-order thinking such as analyzing and synthesizing information. One of the most important goals of information literacy is to create autonomous, lifelong learners.[17] Well-designed libraries can provide spaces for important life skills to be established and continue throughout the phases of life, from childhood to adulthood to retirement. Public libraries are especially important for promoting lifelong learning. This important goal has always been one of the guiding principles of public libraries throughout history.

In the academic library, students come to the library for several different types of experiences to support their learning processes. Well-designed library spaces for learning should contain spaces where students can do collaborative learning, critical thinking, reflection on learning, social construction of knowledge, assessment of learning, and problem-based learning, as well as independent study.[18] Individual students throughout their academic careers may do all of these different types of learning activities at different times and in order to complete varied assignments. Academic libraries can be evaluated by the extent to which they are successful in enabling all kinds of learning in their spaces. With limited resources and funding, it is important that each library determines which functions are the most important for its particular library community. There is a tension in many library spaces between quiet study and collaborative group study. While both kinds of spaces are needed, zoning of library study areas or providing separate floors for quiet and group study can help ease this tension. While good library spaces provide rich materials and technology in addition to study spaces, research shows that most students use the materials that they bring with them when studying in the library.[19] Space is needed to spread out reading materials and books as well as laptops and tablet computers. For this reason, large study tables are often the most popular study spaces, even for individual students studying alone.

Although socializing may be done in the library, the primary focus is on learning, and this makes the library unique from other community spaces. Well-designed library spaces encourage learning by

- supporting both quiet study and social learning,
- emphasizing learning over socializing,
- providing choices of study places for different study preferences,
- allowing students to self-govern their needs in the space, and
- fostering a sense of community and ownership of the space.

While social spaces are valued in the library, studies show that the traditional reading room is still the favorite area for many students. [20] The most important elements to consider when designing academic library spaces to support good pedagogical practices are that the space should be functional, flexible, accessible; provide for a variety of study preferences; be conducive to study; and provide interactivity, as well as being safe, secure, efficient, and environmentally comfortable. Also, appropriate information technology should be provided in library spaces, which includes adequate wiring for plugging in personal computing devices. [21] In addition, library spaces should be designed with accessibility in mind so that libraries are available for safe and convenient use by all constituents and no one is excluded.

## MODERN LIBRARY SPACES

Library spaces today may contain far less books and other physical materials than in the past, but they continue to support teaching and learning through spaces optimized for knowledge gathering and processing. The student-centered spaces of today may also have food and drink available in cafés or vending machines, comfortable and flexible seating, natural lighting, bright colors, artwork, whiteboards, skeletons and other models for study, a variety of technology including Macs and PCs as well as mobile technology checkout, and lots of different places to plug in personal equipment. Student requirements are often the same even between institutions. They desire comfortable, reconfigurable furniture, functional spaces providing multiple learning environments, access to natural light, color and artwork on the walls, and ubiquitous mobile technology. [22] Faculty members are mainly concerned with support for pedagogy and access to resources. Partnerships with academic departments to provide resources, services, and technology for course support are important, and having faculty focus groups to find out specific needs is also a good practice. Providing clear information on what the library can do to support teaching and learning is important since faculty are often unaware of what the library can provide in terms of academic support or they do not consider the library as a full partner in teaching and learning. It's up to librarians to reach out to faculty and show them what we have to offer. For some institutions, this may mean offering community-centered services to support teaching and learning outside the classroom, such as having extended or even 24/7 hours. Building access, security, and cleaning issues arise when considering extended hours. This may increase support costs, which need to be considered by library administrators when planning these services. [23]

The trend over the past few decades is to have less staff posted at a central information desk and to create more self-service and online service points. At the same time, support is increasingly needed for providing access to online resources, research consultations, technology support, and other services. With the growth of e-resources, increased support is needed for helping users find and use these e-resources. This can include virtual spaces such as websites, online tutorials, and web guides, as well as human support in the library. As students and community members are increasingly accessing e-resources through mobile technology, librarians and support staff must become experts in using this technology in order to help community members to access our mobile resources.[24] Another unanticipated result of increased e-resources can be an increased need for printing as students print out online educational materials in order to take notes and because of personal study preferences. Online reading platforms still have a long way to go in order to be conducive to deeper learning and study, so many students still prefer to print out study materials.

The types of library spaces for teaching and learning in today's libraries are varied. Quiet study space may contain the traditional study carrels, small tables, and soft seating in reading areas. Many libraries set up zones in order to keep noisy groups out of quiet areas. Libraries with more than one floor are easier to zone. Glass panels can be installed to zone off quiet study areas without blocking light and at less expense than building walls. Natural zoning can be used to divide quiet learning from collaborative areas. Providing spaces on separate floors can work well to enforce quiet areas as well as provide different types of seating. A popular trend is to remove walls and divide areas with flexible, temporary, or glass walls.[25] Some libraries create glassed-in areas for quiet study rooms or graduates-only reading rooms. Students are typically good at self-policing well-marked quiet study areas without the need for staff intervention. A well-designed study space with designated quiet and conversational areas will help avoid conflicts between the two types of study preferences. Collaborative group study areas can contain a wide variety of group tables, group study rooms, collaboration stations, and soft seating. One of the most popular study areas in many libraries consists of long tables situated near natural lighting where students can study in small groups or individually. Many students in our academic health sciences library express a desire to study individually but near other students where it is "quiet, but not too quiet." Providing a variety of spaces for different learning styles and preferences will assure that the library provides a conducive learning environment for all.

## DESIGN OF LIBRARY SPACES FOR TEACHING AND LEARNING

Libraries need to be designed with the needs of those who will occupy them clearly in mind. Human-centered design is flexible design that meets the needs of individuals. The design of libraries today is moving away from rigid rows of computers in lab spaces to flexible seating with wireless throughout the space in order to accommodate mobile technology. Libraries should be carefully designed to promote optimum learning for the specific needs of the community.[26] The goals of a design project can include updating technological infrastructure to allow for more wireless access, providing areas for support of pedagogy initiatives such as the flipped classroom, providing for technology expertise services, providing access to rich information resources of many kinds, and providing resources and spaces supporting faculty innovation and interdisciplinary research. Goals for student spaces can include creating spaces for constructing knowledge in order to support the constructivist model of learning, providing information access and technology resources, enabling communication through technology, and promoting lifelong learning practices.[27] Spaces can also be designed in a way that promotes interprofessional interactions as well as interactions between diverse groups of people. Well-designed spaces also promote accessibility and are inclusive so that everyone in the community has equal access to learning resources.

Libraries can be the means by which information as well as culture is consumed, created, and shared by individuals, groups, and societies.[28] Library collaboration spaces allow this to happen in academic and community settings. These specially designed spaces advance learning, facilitate communications, build community, and foster relationships. The library has long been thought of as the heart of the academic institution or community. The library of today offers a rich combination of technology, print and electronic resources, service points, and helpful, knowledgeable staff. The service points offered will depend on the community served. Library spaces can bridge the gap between the formal classroom and personal learning spaces. When other community services such as technology experts, writing centers, or student services are located in the library, learning is also enhanced. These types of collaborative community spaces bring innovative new services to people who might not find them in other ways. Collaboration among various community stakeholders in the use of library spaces can help to increase communication and make services more accessible to community members. Integrating supporting services into the library to create one-stop teaching and learning areas can be a very successful strategy for keeping our libraries vital to teaching and learning in our communities.

## TEACHING WITH TECHNOLOGY IN LIBRARY SPACES

The library classrooms of today need to be designed around people, not technologies. They need to be optimized for learning activities, not just trying to pack in as much technology as can fit in the space. Well-designed teaching spaces allow for bringing technology into the space when needed instead of having it already built in, which also allows for constant changes in technology. The emphasis is on flexible use of spaces, and the technology is invisible or at least less prominent than was common in the past. Virtual learning spaces are also important to consider. Websites that provide access to resources, course management systems, e-book platforms, discovery interfaces, web guides, videos, and tutorials are all virtual spaces where the library carries out the teaching and learning role. Virtual learning spaces might include an institutional repository providing access to research or a discovery layer that makes information easier to find, as well as digitization of special collections to increase accessibility of historical or unique resources and access to software and other resources through virtual servers, making these resources available to all community members.

The *learning commons* is a type of space in libraries that was originally designed for students to access technology. Over time, the commons went from rows of computer terminals to more flexible technology spaces where students can use their own computers and mobile devices. As collections become more digital and technology spaces are increasingly needed to access the electronic collections and Internet resources as well as course management systems, library spaces evolve to accommodate these changes.[29] The learning commons idea originally grew out of common areas where faculty and students gathered to discuss and debate in traditional libraries of higher education. With the rise of technology and online information, information commons were created in the 1990s to provide access to computers. These were originally rooms filled with computers in rows, with the teacher standing up front at a presentation station. The goal was access to information and mastery of subject matter.[30] More recently, the learning commons model has changed to accommodate more collaborative learning where students are active participants in the learning process. The new learning commons model is built around the concepts of social learning, student-managed learning, and flexibility in order to accommodate varied learning tasks and to allow for changes in the needs of the community stakeholders. In this revisioned learning commons model, students are creators of information rather than consumers. Currently, a new model is arising in which across campus, learning spaces are even more flexible and responsive to learners' needs. Food services, shared space with other support services, and incorporating activities promoting meaningful experiences in the real world are hallmarks of this new model.[31]

We can look at this evolution of library learning spaces through the SAMR model of evaluating technology innovation, which we explored in chapter 5. At the basic level, a computer lab is created as a substitute (S) for reading books to gather information. Adding multimedia authoring software to these computers to allow for fostering creation of knowledge augments (A) the use of technology making it more transformative. In a learning commons model, the library collaborates with other campus or community units to modify (M) the space in order to serve more departments and services outside of purely library initiatives. Library services become more collaborative and are therefore more transformative. Finally, when the library further aligns with campus-wide initiatives for teaching and learning, such as to support curriculum revision or teaching initiatives such as flipping the classroom, then our spaces become transformed to provide new and truly innovative services, redefining (R) how we teach and learn in library spaces. Library technology spaces need to move from the static provider of information technology to dynamic spaces that provide tools for knowledge creation in ways that bring in cross-campus collaboration.[32]

At the University of Queensland, researchers identified four generations of library spaces. The first generation is collection centric, filled with rows of book stacks, static computer labs, and study carrels. The second-generation library space is more client centered with a service focus. This type of library space has service points centered around helping users to locate and access information. The third-generation library space is focused less on collections and services and more on the user experience and on supporting educational pedagogy. Users are presented with choices of study areas that encourage them to engage with information and interact with multiple types of information resources, including print, digital, and video, as well as with other people, including students, faculty, librarians, and other service providers. These kinds of spaces are the learning commons spaces that many libraries are designing today. The University of Queensland report goes one step further and defines the fourth generation of library spaces as being supportive of "connected learning experiences."[33] These spaces support the pedagogy needs of entire communities, schools, or even campuses. They provide complete learning environments that provide multiple services that are integrated with library and information services. The fourth-generation learning space is highly flexible and involves collaborations with multiple stakeholders. Active learning areas, spaces with support for collaborative group work, and spaces to experiment and create new learning products are provided.

## REDESIGNING LIBRARY SPACES FOR TEACHING AND LEARNING

At the University of Washington (UW), after a large space of over 15,000 feet was freed up by consolidating the library's collection, the library space was converted to an active learning space called the Research Commons. In 2009, when this project started, small branch libraries were being closed and collections were being consolidated. A large space in a centrally located area with a lot of student traffic was converted from a branch library to an active learning space in a relatively short time period. The library's collection was relocated, and the shelving moved out. Existing furniture was reused, as well as tables and seating from other branch libraries. Carrels were set up near windows, a computer workstation and printing area was created near the entrance, and large tables and chairs were brought in for group study, along with smaller tables to accommodate individual and small-group work. Portable whiteboards were added, and an information and technology support desk area was created near the computer area. There were several areas that could also serve as small-group study areas. The space was quickly set up and opened as a pilot program while planning and assessment took place over the next year; see figure 6.1 for the original sketch of the proposed layout.[34]

The original goal of the Research Commons Planning Committee was to support students and faculty in all steps of the research process. The planning committee undertook extensive focus groups and interviews with all stakeholders, including faculty, staff, students, and other potential collaborators, in order to explore the needs and wants of all participants. An in-person survey of users was also conducted in the space. Flipcharts were placed in the area asking for feedback from people using the newly configured space. The committee also did a literature review of library space studies and explored

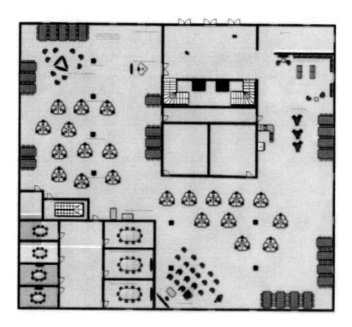

**Figure 6.1. Conceptualized drawing of an open, flexible library learning space**

libraries at other institutions that were reconfiguring their spaces. This was the first active learning space in the UW libraries and filled an unmet need for open, flexible study space partnered with technology and other services.

As a result of the pilot project and with feedback from the many assessment activities, the planning committee came up with several goals for the new space:

- Create an inviting, flexible, collaborative space for research.
- Provide quality staffing and services to support research and study.
- Provide cutting-edge technology in the space.
- Connect people, resources, and tools to facilitate the research process.
- Collaborate with other university departments for integrated services and resources.

Interviews with community stakeholders determined several themes and needs that guided the next phase of the remodel of the space. Some specific needs identified included videoconferencing facilities; collaboration and communication programs to facilitate sharing of research across campus; facilitation of interdisciplinary research; access to specialized software such as GIS, data storage, and statistics packages; tech support staff and spaces equipped with presentation software and hardware to facilitate presentation practice; and a showcase for research and artwork. The physical space needed to incorporate areas for both individual and collaborative group study, including quiet areas and different configurations of comfortable, re-configurable furniture. Collaboration partners for the space included a writing center with research support as well as resources for grant writing. Research classes and professional development for graduate students were also planned to be held in the space. The Research Commons was envisioned as a place where researchers could come to find out about resources and services available across the institution.[35]

The survey of users who visited the space during the pilot period was very helpful in designing the new library space. Many of the survey respondents were undergraduate students, which was surprising since the area was previously a graduate sciences library and a popular undergraduate library is located nearby. Students using the space were from many different departments, some of whom were willing to walk across campus to use the innovative space. The survey found that most respondents used the space two times per week, although there were a few who used the space five times per week. The most common uses of the space were reported to be individual study and computer usage. Only 30 percent indicated they brought their own laptops, and surprisingly few used the area for group study. Computers in the area were most commonly used to search for information, send e-mail, browse the Internet, and print. Students were also asked what kind of services they would like to see provided in the space. The most common requests were for more computers, a café, and more quiet areas. Group study areas were also requested, as well as more outlets for connecting computer equipment. Many requests expressed the need for soft, comfortable furniture and bright colors in the space, as well as artwork on the walls.[36] Over all, the comments about the existing temporary space were very positive, and the numbers of students using the space continued to grow during the pilot period.

Following the pilot study, funding was obtained to remodel the space and bring in new furniture, paint, decorations, and technology. A librarian was hired to manage the day-to-day operations and to create programming for the space. Staff members were reassigned to the area, and office spaces were set up for partners in the space such as the graduate funding office. Today, the space is an active, vibrant, constantly changing teaching and learning space that has continued to be popular with students and hosts numerous events promoting teaching and learning in the university community. There are currently more than 10 cross-university partnerships. Assessment is ongoing. A follow-up survey showed significant changes from the original conception in how the space was used. Funding was found from several sources in order to add seating, upgrade technology, and create high-tech presentation spaces. Workshop series, talks, and posters are presented throughout the year by faculty members, guest speakers, researchers, and students. The online virtual space has a room reservation system and details the equipment available in each space. Past presentations are recorded and accessible from the library's website. The space fills the emerging need for a collaborative environment for students and faculty to come together in order to share research and resources and get support from campus-wide partners, providing for all steps in the research process.

Next-generation learning spaces designed for active learning or "active learning spaces" have been shown to encourage increased engagement for students and also increased interaction between students and with the instructor. Some reports on the use of active learning classrooms find that learning outcomes are increased and students perform better.[37] Some of the major differences between active learning classrooms and traditional classrooms include increased technology provided in the room for teachers and students, group-seating layout, and lack of a central focus point in the room. The instructor is no longer at the head of the room with all students' eyes facing forward. Instructors face the challenge of learning to use a more group-based active learning model in the active learning classroom. It is recommended that instructors practice using the active learning room before teaching their first class in the room and decide which of the room's available learning technologies to use. Figure 6.2 shows the layout of an active learning classroom.

Instructors should communicate expectations and reasons for wanting to use an active learning classroom to their students at the beginning of the course. Students can be asked for feedback on learning in the classroom, and instructors can then make adjustments if needed. The nontraditional class-room setting may be distracting to students. It is helpful to verbally direct their attention to each new activity so that they clearly know where to focus their attention. Intersperse small-group activities with reporting out the re-sults of activities to the whole group in order to break up the format of classroom activities. It's also good to have quiet time when the technology is put away and students can reflect on their learning. Instructors who are new to active learning classrooms and are used to a more traditional lecture ap-proach may need to implement small changes, one at a time, as they get used to teaching in a new way. Students who are used to passively viewing lecture classes may need to be encouraged to participate in small-group activities. The trade-offs are worth it since students working in groups have increased social support, are reported to learn better than students working individual-ly, and report higher satisfaction with learning. [38]

In a recent study of student perceptions of active learning, researchers found that active learning applied in traditional classrooms was not popular with students, while active learning techniques practiced in specially built active learning classrooms were viewed as more successful. Some guidelines for successful use of active learning classrooms include smaller class sizes, high-quality activities done before class to set up the classroom activities,

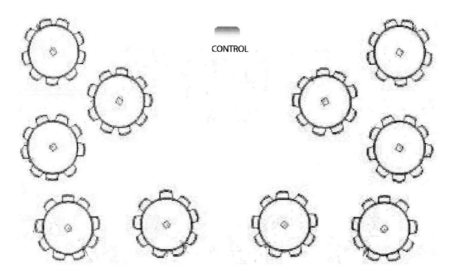

**Figure 6.2.   Conceptualized drawing of an active learning classroom**

well-organized in-classroom activities directed by engaged instructors, and well-trained and well-prepared instructors.[39] This study points out the importance of training instructors in active learning techniques. With training and experience, both instructors and students report enhanced course enjoyment, excitement about learning, and course engagement in active learning classrooms compared with regular classrooms. These outcomes make active learning classrooms desirable despite the cost of creating them and the necessary faculty and staff training in order to use them effectively.

## ASSESSING LIBRARY SPACES

Assessment of library spaces can be done in many ways and should be an ongoing process of continuous improvement. Changes over time in institutional or community needs will make it necessary to reassess library spaces. Assessment can be done though focus groups, in-person or online surveys, or by observational methods. All of these methods can obtain valuable insights into how library spaces are used and help to identify unmet needs. Researchers at Educause and leaders from several leading higher education institutions came together in 2011 to create a system for rating learning spaces. The tool they developed is called the Learning Space Rating System (LSRS) and contains 50 questions organized around 6 important categories.[40] The categories include

- integration with campus context,
- planning process,
- support and operations,
- environmental quality,
- layout and furnishings, and
- technology and tools.

The LSRS is a self-assessment tool and can be used as a guide for remodeling classrooms or constructing new active learning spaces. The current version of the LSRS is intended for formal learning spaces, but a modified tool is being developed for informal spaces. The tool can be used to stimulate conversations during the planning and design process about what an active learning classroom really is and to help identify features and needs that may be missing or need to be reconsidered. Since the cost of creating new learning spaces can be high and the process is complex, using a rating system to meet agreed upon standards of success can be extremely helpful. Using this assessment tool helps ensure that new learning spaces will provide an optimum learning environment that meets the needs of the institution as well as the needs of learners and instructors. More information about the LSRS can be found at www.educause.edu/eli/initiatives/learning-space-rating-system.

One new method increasingly used to assess the usage of library study spaces is borrowed from ethnographic studies. The field of anthropology has long used ethnographic methods to observe the behavior of groups of people in order to document patterns of behavior and tell the story of that particular group.[41] A condensed form of the ethnographic study can be used to study how people use the library space and inform design and redesign of spaces to better fit their needs. The ethnographic method involves researchers observing student behavior in the library in an unobtrusive way. This usually involves taking notes on locations of students and their activities while in the library. It can range from simply noting where students most frequently sit to complex mapping of student movement throughout the library space and taking detailed notes about their study and social behavior.

In an ethnographic study conducted at Loughborough University in the United Kingdom, researchers conducted an ethnographic study of their new open, flexible study space and found several themes.[42] Both group and individual study were popular in the open study space. Groups ranged from 2 to 10 people, and individuals often interspersed themselves among the groups. Groups ranged from quietly studying together to brainstorming and collaborative projects. Brainstorming and group study were often supported by the use of the library's portable whiteboards. Groups using the whiteboards were usually the noisiest. Groups rarely clustered around desktop PCs in the space but preferred to gather around personal laptops. Individuals in the space engaged in silent study of personal materials or writing on their laptops. Individuals rarely used the print materials in the library but studied from their own books and printouts of class handouts and PowerPoint presentations. Both individuals and groups preferred the spaces furthest from the entrance to the library. Spaces near an outside window were especially popular. The PCs at the entrance to the library were used for quickly checking e-mail or printing materials. The entrance to the library space was also used for socializing and making cell phone calls. Students using the space self-policed when noise became too loud but were very tolerant of noise in the space overall, even when studying quietly by themselves. Students often engaged in social activities with friends and used their mobile technology to text, check e-mail, and listen to music while studying. This kind of multitasking seems to be common and did not seem to interfere with learning activities. Most users of the library space were self-sufficient and rarely interacted with library staff or looked for help except for with printing problems.[43] The informal, open space of this library was highly successful with its undergraduate population for its flexible layout and ready access to technology and other services such as a colocated café.

Even in a successful, popular library space, assessment needs to be ongoing, with constant feedback from stakeholders. Building community relationships and institutional partnerships will serve libraries well as they constantly strive to assess spaces and adjust to changing needs and new institutional goals and initiatives. When planning spaces, the big picture needs to be kept in mind, beyond the wants and needs of the community. Needs and wants are important, but the mission and goals of the institution should be in the forefront when thinking about designing spaces.[44] Planning and assessment in the actual spaces to be designed or redesigned are an important consideration. For example, Cal Poly held focus groups in the actual space to be designed so that participants could envision the outcome. They also forged relationships with multiple stakeholders throughout the redesign process and then maintained those relationships in order to assess and reassess the space over time.[45] Design in this way is an iterative process. This allows the facility to be able to respond to new needs or changes in focus in a relatively short time. This flexibility is needed in order to keep our spaces relevant and responsive in the dynamic information world that we currently live in. The dynamic, constantly changing spaces for learning such as those described here require continuous training and learning by library staff as well.

## THE FUTURE OF LIBRARY SPACES

As libraries continue to become more electronic and physical stacks shrink, library spaces are becoming more important to our teaching and learning mission. Active learning classrooms, collaborative study spaces, and innovative services such as three-dimensional printing and video studios are trends to watch for in the future. The next chapter will examine more of these innovative services with which students are creating knowledge products in library spaces, further extending the teaching and learning mission of libraries. Collaborations with other community services and educational support groups within the library space are also an increasing trend. Consciously designing library spaces for the future in order to support teaching and learning will ensure the continued relevance of libraries to institutions and communities. Focusing on the individual library community's specific needs and environment and continually assessing those needs will ensure the library remains the center of the community of learning, now and for future generations.

## NOTES

1. Joan Lippincott, "The Future for Teaching and Learning: Librarians' Deepening Involvement in Pedagogy and Curriculum," *American Libraries*, accessed February 1, 2016, http://americanlibrariesmagazine.org/2015/02/26/the-future-for-teaching-and-learning/.

2. Joanna Bryant, Graham Matthews, and Graham Walton, "Academic Libraries and Social and Learning Space: A Case Study of Loughborough University Library, UK," *Journal of Librarianship and Information Science* 41, no. 1 (2009): 7–18.

3. Scott Bennett, "Learning Behaviors and Learning Spaces," *Portal: Libraries and the Academy* 11, no. 3 (2011): 765–89.

4. Bryant, "Academic Libraries and Social and Learning Space."

5. Ibid.

6. Ibid.

7. Mary M. Somerville and Lydia Collins, "Collaborative Design: A Learner-Centered Library Planning Approach," *Electronic Library* 26, no. 6 (2008): 803–20.

8. Jill Beard and Penny Dale, "Redesigning Services for the Net-Gen and Beyond: A Holistic Review of Pedagogy, Resource, and Learning Space," *New Review of Academic Librarianship* 14, nos. 1–2 (2008): 99–114.

9. David Radcliffe, Hamilton Wilson, Derek Powell, and Belinda Tibbetts, "Designing Next Generation Places of Learning: Collaboration at the Pedagogy-Space-Technology Nexus," University of Queensland (2008).

10. Bennett, "Learning Behaviors."

11. Rachel Applegate, "The Library Is for Studying: Student Preferences for Study Space," *Journal of Academic Librarianship* 35, no. 4 (2009): 341–46.

12. Denise E. Agosto, Jonathan Pacheco Bell, Anthony Bernier, and Meghann Kuhlmann, "'This Is Our Library, and It's a Pretty Cool Place': A User-Centered Study of Public Library YA Spaces," *Public Library Quarterly* 34, no. 1 (2015): 23–43.

13. Ibid.

14. Rebecca M. Sullivan, "Common Knowledge: Learning Spaces in Academic Libraries," *College & Undergraduate Libraries* 17, nos. 2–3 (2010): 130–48.

15. Beard and Dale, "Redesigning Services for the Net-Gen."

16. Pei-chun Lin, Kuan-nien Chen, and Sung-Shan Chang, "Before There Was a Place Called Library—Library Space as an Invisible Factor Affecting Students' Learning," *Libri* 60, no. 4 (2010): 339–51.

17. Beard and Dale, "Redesigning Services for the Net-Gen."

18. Lin, Chen, and Chang, "Before There Was a Place Called Library."

19. Ibid.

20. Ibid.

21. Ibid.

22. Somerville and Collins, "Collaborative Design."

23. Beard and Dale, "Redesigning Services for the Net-Gen."

24. Ibid.

25. Ibid.

26. Somerville and Collins, "Collaborative Design."

27. Ibid.

28. Ibid.

29. Bryan Sinclair, "Commons 2.0: Library Spaces Designed for Collaborative Learning," *Educause Quarterly* 30, no. 4 (2007): 4–6.

30. Somerville and Collins, "Collaborative Design."

31. Sinclair, "Commons 2.0."

32. Somerville and Collins, "Collaborative Design."

33. Radcliffe et al., "Designing Next Generation Places of Learning," 9.

34. University of Washington Libraries, "Research Commons Planning Committee Final Report," unpublished report (2009).

35. Ibid.

36. Ibid.

37. Christina I. Petersen and Kristen S. Gorman, "Strategies to Address Common Challenges When Teaching in an Active Learning Classroom," *New Directions for Teaching and Learning* 2014, no. 137 (2014): 63–70.

38. Ibid.

39. James Juergensen, Tina Oestreich, Brian T. Yuhnke, and Michael Keeny, "New Challenges to Active Learning Initiatives," Educause.com, accessed February 1, 2016, http://er.educause.edu/articles/2016/1/new-challenges-to-active-learning-initiatives.

40. Elliot Felix and Malcolm Brown, "The Case for a Learning Space Performance Rating System," *Journal of Learning Spaces* 1, no. 1 (2011).

41. Bryant et al., "Academic Libraries and Social and Learning Space."

42. Ibid.

43. Ibid.

44. Somerville and Collins, "Collaborative Design."

45. Ibid.

*Chapter Seven*

# Learning through Creating in Library Spaces

It can be argued that the highest form of learning is achieved in creating objects that are meaningful to the creator and that help him or her achieve personal and professional goals. Learning through creating requires spaces that encourage experimentation and provide tools for creation. Social and collaborative spaces, along with supplies and equipment, are needed to facilitate this kind of learning. What better place to provide this kind of learning space than in the library, which is often the center of a community or institution, open to all. Libraries can collaborate along the entire cycle of creation—from idea conception to development, dissemination, and preservation. A spirit of experimentation is essential to creativity. There are no failures in this kind of learning, as every creative activity produces learning, whether the outcome is as expected or not. Physical and virtual spaces for experimental learning in physical and digital formats are both needed. Libraries need to expand their mission beyond helping people to consume information to facilitating the creation of new knowledge and knowledge products. According to an article published in the *Atlantic* in March 2016, the library has long been a place of experimentation. The article states that Ben Franklin conducted some of his experiments with electricity in library spaces. [1] Whether through hosting makerspaces, fabrication labs, or facilitating journal publishing and digital humanities, the library is becoming a hub for creativity and scholarly creation, encouraging the kind of creativity needed in order to produce innovations in art and humanities as well as science and technology.

Beyond mere consumers of education, students today are becoming creators of their own education and knowledge. In a 2009 address at the National Academies of Science, U.S. president Barack Obama stated,

I want us all to think about new and creative ways to engage young people in science and engineering, whether it's science festivals, robotics competitions, fairs that encourage young people to create and build and invent—to be makers of things not just consumers of things.[2]

We need citizens of the future who are well educated in science and technology as well as other disciplines, who are curious and creative and want to solve real-world problems. Science and technology fields in particular have the potential to improve our communities, our health, and our environment. Studies have shown that in elementary education, students are likely to receive less than three hours a week of instruction in science and technology subjects.[3] Science is often taught through reading textbooks and answering problem questions rather than engaging students in real-world problem solving and experimentation, which could inspire a lasting love of science. In order to attract students toward science, problem solving, and creative pursuits, an environment of open experimentation and creativity needs to be encouraged. Libraries can provide this environment and, furthermore, make it available to people from all walks of life and at any age or stage in their lives.

Providing access to tools for creating in the library, beyond any other teaching and learning activity, follows the constructivist model of learning. Making things involves developing ideas, testing, experimenting, and building a physical or digital object. This process embodies the model of constructivist learning, where knowledge is actively constructed by the learner through their experiences.[4] The object created is a representation of the learner's thinking process, which can again lead to the process of developing new ideas and repeating the learning process again. In the arts, studio spaces have long supported the creative process by providing materials and a supportive environment for experimentation and learning new techniques. Tools and materials can be thought of as scaffolding for learning. New forms of studio spaces are now being created for learning in other disciplines besides the arts such as humanities, science, and technology. These spaces are social and collaborative in nature rather than solitary and competitive. Above all, these new learning spaces provide opportunities to create real solutions to real problems and to participate in authentic, real-world activities that are directly related to the learner's life and personal goals.

In addition to teaching information literacy, libraries can promote a new "creative literacy," where users are given the means to transform their ideas into reality through innovative library spaces, both physical and virtual.[5] The places we do these activities can be called *makerspaces* or *centers for publishing* or *video studios*. Increasingly, library spaces are being reconfigured or remodeled to include these new kinds of spaces for teaching and learning. The educational philosophy of a creative learning space is quite different from traditional teaching and learning. In a creation space, students take the lead in their own learning processes and teachers act as guides. Other students may also act as teachers as they mentor their fellow students. Learning is hands-on and problem-based with real-world applications. Students chart their own course in the development of knowledge through the act of creating. This kind of learning environment inspires deep thinking, questioning, and reflection on learning.[6] Teachers facilitate learning by posing questions and providing the tools for learning. This method of learning is highly individualized to each student. When a group of students is challenged to find or build a solution to a problem, each student will approach the problem slightly differently depending on their background, past learning, and personality traits. This type of learning values individuality and personal innovation, which contrasts with traditional education, designed to teach all students to master the same concepts in order to pass a final summative test.

In order to be successful, this type of learning by creation needs to be done in a highly supportive environment where students are free to explore and play without fear of failing. Some guiding principles for creating this type of environment include inviting curiosity, inspiring wonder, and encouraging play.[7] Humans are naturally curious, and we are drawn to learning when questions are posed that invite curiosity. Similarly, when students observe something that causes them to wonder "why," this can stimulate a strong desire to search for answers or solutions. Children learn by playing, and as adults we sometimes become afraid to play with new technology or ideas. A creative learning space encourages learners of all ages to play with tools and materials in unique ways that express individual creativity. In this environment, each student's creative products are valued and recognized. Putting student creations on display can be a strong motivation for learning. True innovation comes about by trying out different solutions until success is reached. Each try may not be perfect, but it is another step toward success, and so there is no "failure" in the sense where traditional education assigns a failing grade. In fact, failure may be encouraged, as learning occurs when something doesn't work out the way it was imagined. Collaborative work and an environment of success are essential to this kind of learning. Working together, individuals may be able to accomplish more than if they were working alone. Sharing knowledge and encouraging each other enables teams of people to solve complex problems and find innovative solutions that might not have been possible for someone working alone.

In the rest of this chapter, we will explore some ways in which libraries are providing creative learning spaces such as data visualization studios, student publication spaces, video studios, makerspaces, digital humanities centers, and online scholarly publishing platforms. Some of these spaces are simple and relatively easy to create by reconfiguring existing library furniture, rooms, and equipment. Other spaces are intentionally designed to meet the specific needs of a community or institution and may be supported by grants or institutional funding. Some of these spaces will last for years, and others will morph into something else after the pilot project is finished. This process in itself is a learning process and one that requires a spirit of experimentation and a willingness to be open to new ways of doing things. The payoffs can be worth the risks, as learning and creativity are increased and community members are engaged in the learning process.

## VISUALIZING DATA

Information visualization is one of the new technologies highlighted in the 2015 *Horizon Report*, which highlights emerging trends in education and technology. This newly emerging field involves enabling researchers to display research results in a way that is easier to understand than raw data.[8] While charts and graphs have been used for a long time to show data in pictorial form, data visualization goes a step further and tells a story about the data. Enabled by creative software such as Piktochart, Tableau, and Datawrapper, information visualization allows creative data communication options that didn't exist just a few years ago. Many visualization tools are available for free or are inexpensive, and some are hosted online. Others such as Tableau are more expensive but also more powerful tools. Libraries can encourage creative visualization of data through the inclusion of these tools on library computers and in computer labs. In addition, some libraries are taking visualization a step further and teaching the use of these tools as well as hosting online websites with guides to using visualization tools. Future developments include three-dimensional (3-D) visualization and interactive graphics. Data visualization spaces help train the next generation of researchers, enable creative student research projects, and provide new ways of looking at data to discover new connections and directions for research. Libraries could also include teaching about information visualization tools when teaching digital and data literacy sessions or through special workshops and training sessions, depending on the audience and interest level of community members.

## PUBLISHING AS PEDAGOGY

Public sharing of student work can be a great catalyst for learning. When students know their work will be displayed or shared online, they are motivated to do their best work. Also, publishing of student work mirrors real-life work experience. Realizing that students learn best from real-life projects, librarians at the University of Michigan partnered with faculty in three unique projects that encouraged student learning through creation and presentation of their work.[9] The first project involved the creation of a student medical journal. Fourth-year medical students signed up for a year-long elective course in which they learned the entire process of publishing a journal, from soliciting articles to contracting and copyright as well as peer review. Medical school faculty and librarians partnered in developing the syllabus for the course and in teaching class sessions. The library hosted the resulting journal through their existing online publishing software. The medical school journal project gave students hands-on experience in publishing and helped them gain real-life experience that prepared them well for future publishing efforts.

The second project highlighted by University of Michigan librarians was an annual event where students read their creative writing and poetry selections in a public library space. This project has been going on for several years, and each year a printed anthology of students' work is produced from the event. The experience of participating in the event takes students through the creative process to actual public performance of their work. Many students also add media to their presentations. Students must sign a contributor's agreement to publish in the anthology, and a headshot and biography are included. The published works go through an editorial process, and students give the library nonexclusive rights to publish their work so that they retain author rights. Finally, the anthology is published online in the institutional repository. Students can see metrics that track download statistics to see the reach of their works. The library also publishes limited copies of the anthology in print. Previously, an Espresso Book Machine was used to create print copies, but librarians found that commercial print copies are actually cheaper and of higher quality.[10]

Another creative project hosted by librarians at the University of Michigan is the hosting of an exhibit focused on highlighting real-life learning. Both faculty and students produced multimedia exhibits showcasing projects that involved reporting on service projects they completed or involved actually creating a live multimedia exhibit. The library not only hosted the exhibits but also provided support for rich media creation. They also recently launched a high-tech design lab in the library to support this project and to enhance engagement with students doing creative projects.[11] The key to their success in these and other projects has been an investment in learning technologies for publishing and creating. The librarians also emphasize the library as a partner with faculty and students in these projects, not just as a service provider. Agreements are created between the partners to clarify expectations and avoid misunderstanding. Costs for publishing are made clear, helping the library to recoup costs and making the programs more sustainable.[12] These innovative projects allow students to gain valuable real-life publishing and exhibition experience beyond traditional learning models. While all of these projects produced successful student publications, it is important to align projects with other programs such as honors colleges, research programs, and for-credit courses in order to encourage sufficient participation to keep the program continuing beyond the first issue or event.

## EDUCATIONAL MAKERSPACES

The creation of educational makerspaces is a movement that has the potential to revolutionize education. Makerspaces embody the ideal of the constructivist model of learning because they enable the physical creation of objects in a hands-on learning environment.[13] All kinds of libraries, including public, academic, and special libraries, are beginning to remodel spaces within the library to enable hands-on learning. Throughout history, humans have been creators; from the invention of the wheel to modern-day space exploration, humans learn by doing and create new and innovative physical objects to make our lives better. The makerspace movement is distinguished by making objects through the use of digital desktop tools, as well as other traditional craft and building materials. Other key characteristics of the maker movement include sharing of designs, online collaboration, and the creation of design standards to enable sharing and fast replication of ideas.[14] In the maker movement, *making* is defined as a set of creative activities, *makerspaces* are communities of creation, and *makers* are the individuals who create in makerspaces. Libraries, which are free and open to an entire community of learners and potential creators, are the ideal environment for makerspaces to exist and thrive in.

The 2015 *Horizon Report* lists makerspaces as on the immediate horizon for whole-scale adoption.[15] Identified by a variety of names, including *makerspaces*, *innovation spaces*, or *fabrication labs*, these learning spaces contain tools and supplies available for designing and creating new products. The equipment provided can range from Legos and sewing kits to 3-D printers. Because of the central location of libraries in a community, they are the perfect setting for these hands-on learning and creating spaces. Higher-order thinking skills and problem solving are engaged when learners work on designing and producing new products and devices. Rooted in real-world applications, students and community members have the opportunity to prototype their creations and possibly produce a marketable new device. Digital tools can also be provided in makerspaces, allowing users to create websites, apps, and games through the use of computer software and hardware. Hackerspaces are another maker activity where computer programmers come together to create new software solutions. Fabrication labs or fab labs are another name for makerspaces that may include engineering tools and 3-D printers. Not just for engineering students, innovation spaces are used by business students, artists, and K–12 students creating science projects, as well as by public library users interested in prototyping new inventions. Because the library serves the entire community, locating a makerspace within the library enables collaboration across disciplines and makes the tools and technology available to everyone.

The following are online resources for those interested in makerspaces and the maker movement:

*MAKE* magazine—http://makezine.com/
MakerEd—http://makered.org/
FabFoundation—www.fabfoundation.org/
FabLab@School—https://tltl.stanford.edu/project/fablabschool
Maker Bridge—http://makerbridge.si.umich.edu/
Harold Washington Library Center Maker Lab—www.chipublib.org/ maker-lab/
Madison Public Library–*Library Makers* blog—http://librarymakers. blogspot.com/
Maker Faire events—http://makerfaire.com/
The Maker Map—http://themakermap.com/
John Burke's Makerspace Resources—www.users.miamioh.edu/burkejj/ makerspaces.html[16]

## 3-D Printing

Three-dimensional printing has been around for many years but has only recently become accessible to the public. In the past, 3-D printing was only available in engineering and manufacturing businesses due to the high cost of the equipment and supplies. Recently, inexpensive 3-D printing models have begun to be mass produced, making this technology more accessible. Three-dimensional printing works by heating plastic or other materials to a liquid form. A computer controls the laying out of thin layers of material, fused to each previous layer and then hardened to form the completed model.[17] The creation of these 3-D models is enabled by software that creates the 3-D file used by the computer to control the printing of the model. The hard part is creating the 3-D file or STL file, which can be created manually through computer-assisted drafting (CAD) or through scanning an object with a 3-D scanner.

In a 2014 article, the author describes the successful implementation of 3-D printing in an academic library. Two MakerBot Replicator 3-D printers were purchased, as well as a 3-D scanner in order to make it easier to create digital models. After spending a couple months calibrating the equipment and experimenting with print quality, the printer was put into production in the library. After the initial setup, the printers required little maintenance. A mediated service was set up due to the length of time it takes to print and the complexity of getting good printing quality. Users submitted 3-D files to

library staff who were trained to operate the printers.[18] Policies and procedures were established, and a small fee was charged by the hour for materials
costs. Users must create their own models, but library staff will consult on
the best ways to print or advise if there are any problems anticipated with
printing a particular 3-D model. The 3-D printing service was displayed at an
open house event in order to market the service. Class sessions were also
conducted to train faculty to use the printers. There was a high rate of repeat
users, suggesting satisfaction with the service.[19] Providing students with access to this emerging technology is an exciting new way for libraries to
enhance teaching and learning in academic institutions. Public libraries are
also implementing 3-D printing, opening up this new technology to all community members.

The University of Washington Health Sciences Library was able to obtain
funding to pilot 3-D printing in the library in 2014. We purchased one of the
original MakerBot 3-D printers and trained technology staff in its use. We
quickly found that quite a bit of expertise was needed to design a 3-D object
that will print correctly on a 3-D printer. There are many 3-D object files
available online from websites such as Thingiverse (www.thingiverse.com),
but creating a 3-D print file from scratch takes a lot more skill with computer
software. We also found that because of the design of the printer, where layer
after layer of material is glued down on top of the previous layer, the objects
sometimes need a base on which to sit. In addition, objects that are not solid
may need to be trimmed of extra filament after printing. Printing objects over
one inch in diameter may take several hours. The plastic filament used to
print the objects has very little waste and is reasonable in price. We did not
charge for the initial pilot program in our library. We decided on a mediated
model of service since most users did not have any previous experience with
3-D printing.

After training technology staff to use our 3-D printer, we set it up in a
dedicated 3-D printing space and advertised its availability to the health
sciences schools. Faculty and students came from many different departments, not just health sciences, to use our printer during the pilot project.
From health sciences, dentistry students were repeat users in order to print
dental models. These usually printed well as long as they had a flat base.
Engineering was a frequent user in order to print models of parts. Several
people tried to print molecules and other biological models, but complex
objects with holes in them do not translate well to 3-D printing. Spatial
models printed well, but it was discovered that wide, flat objects tended to
curl upward on the edges after printing. Several people wanted to print cases
for cameras or phones, which worked well unless they wanted to use them
outside since the material used for 3-D printing is biodegradable and will
break down in water.

After several months of usage, our MakerBot extruder nozzle broke down due to a design flaw of the particular model we purchased, so we ended the pilot project. There are replacement print heads available for this model, but it is difficult to get them from the manufacturer at this time. Out of 63 print jobs requested during the pilot project, there was a 60 percent success rate. Some designs were not suitable for printing, others didn't scale well or the print material was not suitable for the object being printed. Besides academic usage, several users experimented with using the 3-D printer for personal projects. There are now two other 3-D printers in another library on campus, so we have not yet replaced our MakerBot. Also, our library does not have good air circulation in the room where 3-D printing was done. Three-dimensional printers can give off fumes and require good ventilation in order to protect the operators. Figure 7.1 shows the MakerBot printer and some 3-D printed objects.

## VIDEO STUDIOS AND PRESENTATION PLACES

Presentation and video studios have become popular in library spaces over the past several years. They fill many needs, such as working on class pres-

**Figure 7.1.   MakerBot 3-D printer and printed objects**

entations, creating videos for course assignments, practicing for job seeking or presentations at conferences, and practicing for dissertation defense.[20] Faculty members may also use the space for recording lectures to be posted in online courses. Many libraries are converting old study rooms or class-rooms to interactive presentation studios. Funding for technology can many times be obtained through small grant programs on campus or through edu-cational technology improvement awards. Many campuses have student technology fee grants they can tap into to fund a remodel of technology spaces. The cost of a presentation space depends on the equipment needed. A computer and projector with Microsoft Office software plus video production software is usually essential. An interactive whiteboard such as the Smart Board with built-in projector can add interactivity to the space. Video, audio, and recording equipment can also be provided, as well as lighting and a green screen if recording will be done in the room. All of our library computers are also equipped with security software that returns the computer to its former state when logged off in order to avoid corrupted software and keep mainte-nance to a minimum. Depending on the complexity of the equipment pro-vided, staff may need to be on hand to help students or faculty using the room. Staff training is also essential.

At Pennsylvania State University, hardware developers went one step further and created a "one-button" video studio.[21] The hardware and software are bundled together so that users just insert a flash drive and press a button to start recording. Developers created the studio in 2013 after realizing that video creation was becoming more common for student assignments. Faculty and staff also use the video studios. With a growing emphasis on online education, faculty members are looking to enhance teaching and learning by creating videos. The one-button studio works by connecting the lighting, audio, and camera so that only one button is needed to start recording to the flash drive. Lighting position, camera settings, and audio settings are already preconfigured. The system also automatically writes to a flash drive, similar to the common scanning stations already in use in many libraries. The studio is located within the library in order to be available to all users in a central location. The one-button studio is now available at several locations, and developers envision it expanding to public libraries, where students enrolled in online courses as well as other community members could have free access to quality recording equipment for a variety of needs.[22]

In creating a presentation studio or video studio, it's important to develop use policies to protect the equipment and make sure it's available to all users. Some rooms are checked out through online study-room booking software, and some are first come, first served. It may be a good idea to keep the room locked if it is not under constant observation and keep a key at the informa-tion desk to be checked out when reserving the room. Having the room near to computer technology support staff is important if the equipment is not automated, and help may be needed for users to get started. Creating online and print help materials and setup guides is also helpful. Some libraries create online tutorials to help presentation-studio users get started.[23] Marketing the studio is important, as is keeping usage statistics. Assessment should be done to make sure the studio is meeting the needs of the community of users. New equipment or optional attachments and cables may be needed to meet user needs and requests. If the room is large enough, it could be equipped with a table and chairs, making it double as a collaborative space that could also include videoconferencing equipment. Booking software and time limits on room usage may be needed if the room becomes a popularly used space.

A basic list of equipment to create a video studio might include:

- video camera;
- miscellaneous camera equipment: lenses, cables for downloading video, SD card;
- microphone(s);
- tripod;
- green screen, frame, and clips;
- computer with video-processing software;
- floodlights;
- personalized banner/backdrop;
- miscellaneous cables;
- production hardware such as an H.264 recorder and encoding software; and
- whiteboard or Smart Board with projector.

The total cost of a video studio depends on the quality and type of equipment purchased. See figure 7.2 for an example setup. For more information, see the suggested and optional equipment listed on the Penn State One Button Studio setup guide—http://onebutton.psu.edu/setup.[24]

## SUPPORTING DIGITAL HUMANITIES

People engaged in digital humanities work can be said to be creating new knowledge products through research, analysis, and visualization.[25] This process is facilitated and disseminated through digital technologies. Digital humanities involves applying computer technology to arts and humanities as well as exploring new ways of doing scholarship in a digital world. Digital humanities faculty members are introducing more visual, interactive, and technology-driven scholarship into their teaching practices. Students are also involved in the creation of these new knowledge products. Digital humanities

**Figure 7.2.  Basic equipment for a video studio**

is a much more interactive and constructivist way of learning than the traditional lecture model. A broad range of arts and humanities departments are participating in digital humanities and discovering new ways to teach and learn with digital scholarship. Some activities that fit the definition of digital humanities scholarship include:

- building digital collections for scholarly publication or teaching;
- creating new tools for building digital collections;
- creating tools for analyzing and managing digital collections;
- creating new scholarship by analyzing existing digital collections;
- teaching digital humanities to faculty, students, or community members;
- offering spaces for experimentation and innovation in digital humanities; and
- providing repositories and other technology solutions to support digital collections.[26]

Many libraries are already participating in this exciting new field, offering one or more of these services, depending on the needs of their community members.

Centers for digital humanities have been popping up all over for the past decade or so. These are interdisciplinary scholarship centers promoting digital humanities and are physically located in libraries or other academic sites as well as on websites such as HASTAC (www.hastac.org/).[27] The Humanities, Arts, Science, and Technology Alliance and Collaboratory (HASTAC) was created in 2002 in response to concerns about teaching and learning in the humanities and keeping up with an advanced technological society. Centers for digital humanities arose in response to a perceived need for a collaboration of scientists, technologists, and humanists to work together to create new ways of learning in our increasingly global and technology-based society.

In a 2013 study of digital humanities and libraries, the author found that about half of digital humanities centers located in the United States are located within library spaces. Another quarter of the centers are not located in a library but maintain a partnership with the library. While it's estimated that fewer than 10 percent of libraries host a dedicated center for digital humanities, it's much more common for libraries to provide some services such as consulting, technology support, or project management in support of digital humanities.[28] Libraries often have the cross-disciplinary reach to support campus digital humanities efforts as well as the necessary technology infrastructure already in place. Projects hosted in the library may be more sustainable than those hosted by one department in isolation. Some of the traditional work of librarians crosses over into skills needed for digital humanities, especially the work of librarians embedded in humanities departments. Other work such as data management, partnering on scholarship, digitization and curation of materials, as well as digital preservation efforts, discovery of information in a variety of formats, and dissemination of information to users is needed in digital humanities work.

While there are many ways that libraries and librarians can facilitate digital humanities, not every way is right for every library. It is important to work closely with faculty and community members in order to determine the best ways to support those who are actively engaged in teaching and learning in the digital humanities. Faculty members who are working in the field of digital humanities are engaging students in new forms of scholarship that are technologically rich and digital in nature. Public library staff engage in digital humanities work as well when they participate in the preservation or curation of local history, digitization of artworks, or digitization of local documents in order to make them more accessible to the public. Training is needed for those creating digital works as well as those accessing these new forms of scholarship. Librarians can take the lead in working to make digital forms of scholarship more accessible and discoverable as well as working on ways to track faculty output in this new, born-digital form of scholarship.

## Role of the Library in Digital Humanities

Libraries need to keep up with new and emerging researcher needs by supporting born-digital research; each library will need to decide what to support based on their unique mission and stakeholder needs. Libraries' roles vary throughout the research process.[29] One role that is growing quickly is that of managing research data. Some libraries provide data management computing resources and some provide consulting services for researchers needing to find best practices for data management. Other libraries collect data sources for researchers and help organize data. Understanding the researcher's needs and providing the right support at individual institutions is key. The embedded librarian who works closely with researchers, typically in the space where the researchers work, learns to understand researcher needs and research practices in order to provide services that are relevant and timely. Libraries are also positioned to provide digitization and curation services to scholars who are creating content as well as to provide digital preservation of digital scholarship, which may exist in many formats. In addition, libraries are well placed to provide publication and discovery services to disseminate research and scholarly output as well as to track the impact of these new forms of scholarship.

## Challenges of Supporting Digital Humanities in Libraries

Library support of digital humanities does not come without challenges. First of all, there needs to be a robust technology infrastructure to support digital humanities; it is also necessary to provide the administrative support for this type of role. Many times, faculty members are the ones who approach the library for support with digital humanities projects. Librarian-initiated projects should also be encouraged. Both kinds of projects will be collaborative in nature. Librarians offer the infrastructure and skills to get the projects done successfully, while scholars offer the disciplinary knowledge. Training of librarians in digital technologies is needed, and trained librarians are in demand.[30] Online training exists for many of the technologies that may be needed as far as programming languages and web technologies. Project-management skills are also important. Training specifically for librarians may not be offered, but there are many online courses on technology subjects offered from public and private institutions. It may be difficult to identify the specific skills needed to support digital humanities previous to starting a project. Library technology staff are important in supporting these initiatives. It may be hard to justify beginning a digital humanities project in the library when staff members are overworked with their traditional roles in collections, reference, outreach, and instruction. Resources needed for a digital humanities project may be hard to find as well as expensive. Grants and awards supporting these types of projects are increasingly available, but it is a risk to jump into a new area, and justifying that risk may be hard. Justifying the purchase and upkeep of technology and infrastructure in order to support digital humanities may also be difficult. As with all good experimentation, some efforts may fail. Library administrators may be focused on the core mission of the library and reluctant to risk embarking on a costly new project.[31]

In spite of these risks, many libraries have embarked upon digital humanities projects and are successfully supporting the digital humanities at their institutions. For example, the Digital Humanities Incubator at the University of Maryland Libraries and the Scholars' Lab at the University of Virginia are supporting digital humanities.[32] The University of Maryland received a Mellon Grant to support their digital humanities projects in African American history and culture.[33] The grant provides training to faculty, students, staff, and librarians in order to enable them to run workshops, deliver public programming, digitize archival materials, support further research, and integrate digital works into teaching and learning with programs such as the university's first-year innovation and research experience program. At the University of Virginia, the Scholars' Lab (http://scholarslab.org) supports project incubation and graduate training in doing digital humanities and also provides for experimental humanities through providing a makerspace.[34] Training and technology to support geospatial scholarship is also provided through the Scholars' Lab. A digital scholarship services librarian partners with developers, faculty, and other specialists in providing this cross-disciplinary research hub.[35]

## Creating Tools for Digital Humanities

A recent study of digital humanities centers in the United States found that centers can be divided into two main categories: centers created in a physical location and those organized around providing a resource or tool located in a virtual space.[36] Centers located in interdisciplinary spaces such as libraries or museums are more successful and sustainable than those located within individual departments. Also, libraries and museums offer technology infrastructure that may be beyond the means of individual projects. Centers often develop new tools for working with data and resources. These tools are sometimes made freely available to others, but unfortunately studies show that these tools are often not well advertised and are hard to find on center websites.[37] Some tools that have been developed for digital humanities have gone on to be widely used, such as Zotero (an online reference manager), Omeka (web-publishing software for digital exhibits), and ScholarPress (a courseware plug-in for WordPress). Many others were not developed any further after the project finished. Sustainability and continued staffing and maintenance of these digital tools is an issue. There are increasing numbers of grants available for encouraging digital humanities projects from organizations such as the National Endowment for the Humanities and the Mellon Foundation. Tools created for projects funded by these and other foundations for the humanities are often made available as open source products after their development. A group of librarians, historians, and other digital humanities faculty members maintains a website of digital research tools called the Digital Research Tools (DiRT) Directory (http://dirtdirectory.org/).[38]

Digital humanities can cross over into other disciplines as well. At Stony Brook University Health Sciences Library, we decided to create an online exhibit from a physical exhibit of historical dental implements hosted in the library. The physical exhibit was composed of a set of three cases of historical dental tools and implements located in our library's entrance area. We were lucky to have a very talented library intern who had museum experience to take on the work of photographing all of the objects in the exhibit and organizing and creating the metadata for each of the objects. We used Omeka software (http://omeka.org) to publish the photographs and metadata to the web. Omeka includes the option of providing a map indicating the location of each item and allows for multiple views of the items. Digitizing the exhibit allowed many more people to have access to these important historical implements than just the few people visiting the physical exhibit in person. Using the Omeka software, which is open source, made the process of publishing the collection to the web relatively simple.

## SCHOLARLY PUBLISHING IN THE LIBRARY

Many libraries and librarians who feel strongly about open access initiatives and scholarly publishing are getting involved in academic publishing. There is a range of activities that libraries can participate in using both physical library spaces for publishing services and virtual spaces for access to online journals and books, as well as supporting born-digital media. Many libraries are establishing online digital repositories or web portals to hold preprints of scholarly publications from institutional or community sources. Some libraries that have identified a community need for publication hosting have established journal or book publishing services. These publications can range from informal student publications to formal academic journals with a subscription model and academic presses that publish monographs.[39] The range of services offered depends on the needs of the community and the resources available to the library to support the endeavor. Staff time and training are challenges to be weighed against the need for the service. Librarians already have the metadata and cataloging skills to bring to the table, as well as knowledge of scholarly publishing. Scholarly publishing support can be introduced in tiers from offering guidelines and consulting services to helping authors understand their rights and introducing open access to the community. Some libraries also collaborate with faculty in one or more steps in the publishing process. A few libraries are identifying publishing as a core library service and creating publishing centers in the library such as the Center for Digital Research and Scholarship at Columbia University. [40] Some academic institutions are integrating their publishing services with teaching and learning by involving students in working on journal publishing as a teaching tool. In Canada, electronic publishing was given a boost by the Synergies Canada project, which encouraged migrating Canadian journals from print to electronic format. This project led to several universities formally integrating journal publishing into the curriculum along with the establishment of new online journals hosted by the library. [41]

In an article about library publishing services and how they facilitate and help shape scholarly communication, the authors found that over half of the Association of Research Libraries (ARL) member libraries provided some kind of scholarly publishing services. [42] Libraries can help authors, editors, students, and teachers with services such as copyright advising, digitization, intellectual property, and facilitating scholarly communication. These services can be formal or informal, depending on the levels of staff expertise, priorities, and needs of the community members. Librarians participating in the community and sharing ideas about scholarly publishing as well as introducing new forms of communications can drive an institution forward toward more open access models of scholarly communication. Library contributions to scholarly communication can be classified into four main categories: registration, archiving, certification, and awareness. [43] Individual libraries may choose to focus on one or several of these endeavors. Registration activities can include intake of preprints into an institutional repository, assigning a permanent digital object identifier (DOI) to the resource, and making it available to the community and beyond. Some libraries also provide ISSN and ISBN registration services. If the digital object is a journal, libraries may also help publishers submit the title to vendors for indexing or to the Directory of Open Access Journals (DOAJ). The archiving function is a traditional library activity that ensures the long-term preservation of scholarship, whether in print or digital format. Certification refers to the peer-review process and promoting open access publishing as a valid form of academic scholarship. Awareness refers to the activities that libraries provide that make digital scholarship more accessible and discoverable to the public.

## PARTNERING WITH EXPERTS FOR SOFTWARE TRAINING

Not all projects need to have librarian expertise in house or require the purchase of high-tech equipment. Many libraries already partner in teaching and learning initiatives by hosting training in library spaces. By collaborating with faculty and other instructional staff, the library can offer many types of educational programs, depending on the needs of the community. For example, at the University of Washington, we offer statistics software programs on the computers in our teaching classrooms and partner with global health faculty members and graduate assistants who teach multiple sections per quarter, instructing students on how to collect and manipulate research statistics. Recently, we also partnered with our institutional information technology department to host sessions on creating data visualizations using the Tableau software. In this way, we support the creation of data visualizations, from gathering statistics to creating the visual output that helps communicate research in a graphical way so that it is more understandable. Through partnerships, the library can offer creative teaching and learning in library spaces to meet the varied needs of faculty, students, staff, researchers, and community members.

## ASSESSMENT OF CREATION SPACES

In order to provide successful programs that allow people to get creative in library spaces, it's important to fully assess the needs of the library community. A comprehensive program of surveying the changing needs of the community on a regular basis is important. Allowing for suggested services either in the library space or online through a suggestion-box form is a great way to solicit new ideas. When considering specific new projects, focus groups of stakeholders and potential users are crucial to understanding the needs and scope of the project before getting started, especially when there is a possible investment in expensive equipment. Working groups composed of all stakeholders can be formed to shepherd the project from start to finish. These groups can be maintained to continue assessing the project even after it has started to make sure it stays relevant and adjusts to changing needs. Involving stakeholders in steering committees and working groups is also important in order to get their buy-in and promote excitement about the project. Libraries that have librarians embedded in the community or within academic departments often have an advantage in working closely with stakeholders who can help identify teaching and learning needs that the library might provide solutions for using library creation spaces.

## THE FUTURE OF CREATING IN LIBRARY SPACES

Libraries around the world are adapting and reconfiguring library spaces in order to accommodate innovative, creative learning projects in partnership with institutions and community organizations. The forms that these projects take are as variable as the institutions and community organizations that host them. In the future, learning through creating new knowledge products in the library may involve animation, virtual reality, and gaming, as well as other technologies as yet undiscovered. Librarians who are open to experimentation and see a need for creative learning spaces should consider partnering with community members to set aside part of the library for creative pursuits. Funding may be obtained by exploring some of the grants available from humanities-related foundations and trusts or from other local institutions. Setting up spaces for learning by creating in the library increases access to innovative tools like 3-D printers, video equipment, creative software, and publishing platforms, encouraging more innovation and creativity in people of all walks of life and of all ages.

## NOTES

1. Deborah Fallows, "How Libraries Are Becoming Modern Makerspaces," *Atlantic*, accessed March 11, 2016, www.theatlantic.com/technology/archive/2016/03/everyone-is-a-maker/473286/.

2. Margaret Honey and David E. Kanter, eds., *Design, Make, Play: Growing the Next Generation of STEM Innovators* (New York: Routledge, 2013), p. 1.

3. Ibid.

4. Kimberly Sheridan, Erica Rosenfeld Halverson, Breanne Litts, Lisa Brahms, Lynette Jacobs-Priebe, and Trevor Owens, "Learning in the Making: A Comparative Case Study of Three Makerspaces," *Harvard Educational Review* 84, no. 4 (2014): 505–31.

5. Sharona Ginsberg, "3D Printing and Creative Literacy: Why Maker Culture Benefits Libraries," *Everything You Wanted to Know about Information Literacy but Were Afraid to Google*, ed. Kristin Fontichiaro (Ann Arbor, MI: Author, 2012).

6. R. Steven Kurti, Debby L. Kurti, and Laura Fleming, "The Philosophy of Educational Makerspaces: Part 1 of Making an Educational Makerspace," *Teacher Librarian* 41, no. 5 (2014): 8.

7. Ibid.

8. L. Johnson, S. Adams Becker, V. Estrada, and A. Freeman, *NMC Horizon Report: 2015 Library Edition* (Austin, TX: New Media Consortium, 2015), accessed September 30, 2015, http://cdn.nmc.org/media/2015-nmc-horizon-report-library-EN.pdf.

9. Laurie Alexander, Jason Colman, Meredith Kahn, Amanda Peters, Charles Watkinson, and Rebecca Welzenbach, "Publishing as Pedagogy: Connecting Library Services and Technology," *Educause Review*, accessed March 15, 2016, http://er.educause.edu/articles/2016/1/publishing-as-pedagogy-connecting-library-services-and-technology.

10. Ibid.

11. Ibid.

12. Ibid.

13. Kurti, Kurti, and Fleming, "Philosophy of Educational Makerspaces."

14. Erica Rosenfeld Halverson and Kimberly Sheridan, "The Maker Movement in Education," *Harvard Educational Review* 84, no. 4 (2014): 495–504.

15. Johnson et al., *NMC Horizon Report*.

16. John J. Burke, *Makerspaces: A Practical Guide for Librarians* (Lanham, MD: Rowman & Littlefield, 2014).

17. Steven Pryor, "Implementing a 3D Printing Service in an Academic Library," *Journal of Library Administration* 54, no. 1 (2014): 1–10.

18. Ibid.

19. Ibid.

20. Kathryn W. Munson and Karen E. Jung, "Setting the Stage for a Presentation Studio," *Louisiana Libraries* 72, no. 2 (2009): 27–30.

21. Heather Herzog, "Lights, Camera, Action! One Button Studio Offers Video Production with Ease," *Penn State News*, accessed March 15, 2016, http://news.psu.edu/story/283150/2013/07/31/academics/lights-camera-action-one-button-studio-offers-video-production.

22. Ibid.

23. Munson and Jung, "Setting the Stage."

24. Pennsylvania State University, One Button Studio Project website, accessed March 15, 2016, http://onebutton.psu.edu.

25. Chris Alen Sula, "Digital Humanities and Libraries: A Conceptual Model," *Journal of Library Administration* 53, no. 1 (2013): 10–26.

26. Ibid.

27. Humanities, Arts, Science, and Technology Alliance and Collaboratory, HASTAC website, accessed March 15, 2016, www.hastac.org/.

28. Sula, "Digital Humanities and Libraries."

29. Ben Showers, "Does the Library Have a Role to Play in the Digital Humanities?" *JISC Digital Infrastructure Team*, accessed March 15, 2016, https://infteam.jiscinvolve.org/wp/2012/02/23/does-the-library-have-a-role-to-play-in-the-digital-humanities/.

30. Miriam Posner, "No Half Measures: Overcoming Common Challenges to Doing Digital Humanities in the Library," *Journal of Library Administration* 53, no. 1 (2013): 43–52.

31. Ibid.

32. Ibid.

33. University of Maryland, "$1.25 Million Mellon Grant Awarded to UMD's Arts and Humanities College," UMD Right Now, July 15, 2015, accessed March 15, 2016, http://umdrightnow.umd.edu/news/125-million-mellon-grant-awarded-umds-arts-and-humanities-college.

34. University of Virginia Library, Scholars' Lab website, accessed March 15, 2016, http://scholarslab.org/.

35. Ibid.

36. Diane Zorich, *A Survey of Digital Humanities Centers in the United States* (Washington, DC: Council on Library and Information Resources, 2008).

37. Ibid.

38. Digital Research Tools Directory, DiRT Directory website, accessed March 15, 2016, http://dirtdirectory.org.

39. Anali Maughan Perry, Carol Ann Borchert, Timothy S. Deliyannides, Andrea Kosavic, Rebecca Kennison, and Sharon Dyas-Correia, "Libraries as Journal Publishers," *Serials Review* 37, no. 3 (2011): 196–204.

40. Columbia University, Center for Digital Research and Scholarship website, accessed March 15, 2016, http://cdrs.columbia.edu/cdrsmain/.

41. Maughan Perry et al., "Libraries as Journal Publishers."

42. Ji-Hong Park and Jiyoung Shim, "Exploring How Library Publishing Services Facilitate Scholarly Communication," *Journal of Scholarly Publishing* 43, no. 1 (2011): 76–89.

43. Ibid.

## Chapter Eight

# The Future of Teaching and Learning in Libraries

Teaching and learning in libraries has changed drastically with the advent of the digital age and continues to change at a rapid rate. Twenty-first-century learning is social, participatory, and collaborative. Students today need to be engaged in learning, and this happens best when learning is active and experiential. Learners need to explore topics that are relevant and question driven. Learning should be purposeful and project related in order to be relevant to real life. Projects are often interdisciplinary in nature, engendering new directions and undiscovered topics of research. Learning is also reflective, and students need time to think and integrate new knowledge. Many times, this process happens outside the classroom and in library spaces. Twenty-first-century learning is empowering to learners.[1] This kind of learning is creative and motivates students to persevere and learn more. Teachers are no longer experts but guides on the side who provide the tools and frameworks for learning by doing.

In the 21st-century library, the people who use our libraries to learn and find information need to be the center of our work. Collections are no longer the most important part of the library, especially physical collections. Many libraries are beginning to transition to completely virtual collections, and some have already made that transition. For other libraries, that transition may not happen until many years in the future. The shape our libraries take, now more than ever, needs to depend on our individual communities' needs. In academic libraries, librarians are striving to be seen as educators alongside faculty, supporting each other in communities of practice. The academic library must align itself with the educational mission of the institution and become a full partner in that mission in order to remain relevant in the future academic environment. Students are also partners in the library of the future, helping to revision its services and working alongside librarians on student-centered projects. Student works and publications are highlighted and promoted throughout the library. Public libraries are also partners with their communities, and services change as needs change. The library of the future practices continuous assessment in order to stay relevant and responsive to change. [2]

The environment that our libraries exist in today is radically different from the past. Information is no longer scarce, and it is freely available from a wide variety of sources outside of libraries. Information is now available in multiple formats and on multiple types of continuously changing technology. The Google age opens up information to everyone, but the Internet and proliferation of web tools make it easy for just about anyone to become an "expert" and post information to the web. Studies have shown that students today often settle for "good enough" information, rarely searching beyond the first few hits brought up by Google. They rarely check the source of the information they find and tend to bounce around from one source to another. They search quickly using textual search statements that return a lot of material that has to be sorted through, and they read quickly and reject a lot of what they find. [3] This is the environment that libraries today are dealing with, and it is causing transformational change in our methods of teaching and learning, in the tools we use to communicate and instruct, and also in our physical spaces.

In an article on the challenges of libraries today, Tony Horava proposes that libraries reevaluate their strategic plans and explore how to best to serve their communities in ways that may be very different than in the past. [4] Besides shrinking budgets, libraries face new student learning expectations and accommodations to multiple learning styles, the rise of social media, a growing variety of scholarly publication platforms, mobile access to resources, open access initiatives, and constantly changing technology. [5] This requires librarians to be flexible and open to new ways of providing services. Deciding which initiatives to support and what services to stop providing in order to keep up with budget cuts can be a difficult challenge.

Libraries may be faced with doing less and doing some things well enough rather than to the level of quality that may have been provided in the past. For example, some libraries have stopped binding paper journals and may even stop checking them in to save staff time. Cataloging is being outsourced or brief cataloging is being done for some materials. In teaching and learning, we find that with limited staffing it is impossible to reach all students when teaching information literacy. We need to have some measurement of what is considered effective enough for our institutional needs. [6] Assessment of services and outreach to stakeholders is important so we can find out community expectations and needs and to help us make tough choices about what initiatives to support and what services to decrease or discontinue altogether. Staff energy, training, and focus need to be on those activities that will have the greatest impact and offer the highest value to the institution. These decisions require vision and courage from our library leaders

## THE VALUE OF THE LIBRARIES OF THE FUTURE

In a research study of PhD students' usage of the library, researchers recommended reaching out to graduate students working toward their PhD degrees in order to create favorable views of the library, which they will carry with them when they later become faculty members. The study found that undergraduates and even graduates doing regular coursework rely on Google and do not use library services or resources much, except for visiting the physical space to study. Graduate PhD students, on the other hand, need to do more in-depth research as well as cross-disciplinary research that often requires reaching out to librarians for help. Students in the study who had worked with a librarian in the past then valued the library more as measured by a survey instrument used in the research study.[7]

The measurement of library value has changed over the years from the number of books held as an indicator of quality to how many dollars are spent on online resources. Recently, the focus has changed again to measurements of return on investments and user satisfaction. Today, libraries are more concerned with demonstrating their value by measuring impact on library users. This requires setting outcome goals and analyzing the audience served in order to focus librarian time and effort on the specific goals and audiences that will have the most impact. The study of PhD student use of the library indicates that libraries serving PhD-level students would do well to invest librarian time and energy into instruction and outreach with these particular students, who will then value the library more when they become faculty members. In the future, it will be more important for individual libraries of all types to determine the services and resources that will have the most impact and be of the greatest value to their unique community members.

The academic library especially will face many challenges in the future. Changes in higher education will drive changes in academic libraries, so it is imperative for librarians to keep up with higher education trends such as those reported by the *NMC Horizon Report*. It is also imperative to keep up with the strategic directions of parent institutions and to align library strategic plans with the greater institution's vision and goals. In a recent article on the changing roles of academic libraries in the digital age, the author expressed his belief that while the traditional role of the library in education is declining, there is a shift toward the information professional becoming the "library" of the future.[8] In other words, librarians themselves, rather than the library building, will become the focus of the information profession.

Librarians of the future will serve as navigators of knowledge and teachers of information fluency who act as catalysts for learning. They will do this from within classrooms, labs, and the community instead of in the physical library building. The community of learners whom we serve as information professionals will also become increasingly global as virtual learning spaces become more prevalent. Some of the changes brought by the digital age include the need for instruction in e-literacy, personalization of the teaching and learning environment, more responsive learning, increasing open access of literature and data, and new technologies that are context aware and sensor enabled in order to provide information seamlessly at the point of need.[9] Library spaces will become intellectual gathering places to exchange ideas, collaborate, and create knowledge products. Libraries will become more like communities of learning, and community partnerships will enliven and expand our services and resources. The libraries of the future will continue their mission to preserve information in a multitude of formats but will also be full participants in creating new knowledge and knowledge products.

K–12 education is also going through major changes that will affect the future of school libraries. Over the years, there have been many waves of educational reform, such as the 2001 No Child Left Behind legislation. These initiatives have had varying results in educational outcomes but have also led to some undesirable practices such as standardized testing and "teaching to the test." One of the newest reforms currently impacting many U.S. states is the adoption of the "common core" standards. The standards are closely aligned with preparing students for college and careers. Other goals include establishing higher-order thinking skills and preparing students to participate in an increasingly global society. The standards build on current state standards and are meant to be evidence based.[10] Library education is crucial to establishing higher-order thinking skills, and there is also substantial evidence in the literature for the importance of teaching information literacy for future performance both at college and in careers. Close reading of text materials is also stressed in the common core, which has implications for libraries. While K–12 educators are still figuring out the full implications of the implementation of common core standards to teaching and learning practices, school librarians have the opportunity to advocate for having a voice at the table in deciding the future of our children's education.

Public libraries are not exempt from the challenges facing academic and school libraries. Public libraries in the United States serve the widest variety of patrons out of all the different kinds of libraries. All ages attend our public libraries, from preschoolers to senior citizens, new immigrants, and the unemployed looking for jobs, as well as K–12 students and adults doing research or just looking to read a good book. In a study of the New York public libraries, it was found that more visitors come to the New York libraries than all those attending New York professional sports events, museums, arts events, gardens, and zoos combined.[11] For fiscal year 2015, the city libraries had a reported 37 million visitors.[12]

Especially in the world's largest cities, public libraries are highly valued for their resources as well as services such as language classes, computer access, research materials, and other community programs.[13] While library usage remains high, budgets have been shrinking or remain static. The Center for an Urban Future study found that New York public libraries fall behind many other large cities in the number of hours branch libraries are open during the week (see figure 8.1).[14] This especially impacts working adults who need to use the library during the evening and weekend hours. Due to public outcry and librarian activism, fiscal year 2016 will see an additional $43 million in operating funds in order to open the city's libraries for more hours and purchase more library materials. In addition, a commitment has been made to find funds to renovate and modernize library buildings across the city.[15] This historic allocation will allow libraries that have been experiencing years of budget cuts to finally begin to plan for the future.

## PLANNING FOR THE LIBRARIES OF THE FUTURE

In order to deal with the massive changes going on in libraries today, a variety of planning tools are being employed. Some of these tools, such as SWOT analysis, have been used in the business world for many years. The SWOT analysis method involves identifying the strengths, weaknesses, op-

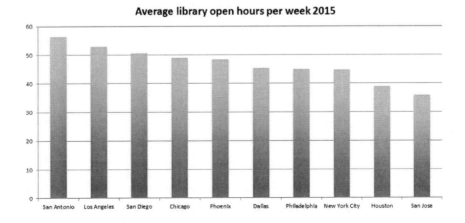

**Figure 8.1. Average large-city library hours (Center for an Urban Future, 2015)**

portunities, and threats facing an institution. This process helps leaders become clear about the environment they are working in and helps them to clarify the audience as well as the services needed for that audience in order to plan for the future.[16] Environmental scanning is another method of identifying trends that can affect library services in the future. The *NMC Horizon Report* is a good example of an environmental-scanning report that is focused on emerging technology in education.

The 2016 *Horizon Report* identifies several trends that are transforming education today. One major trend is creating changes in college and university programs in order to encourage students to be more agile, adaptable, and inventive in order to compete and thrive in the modern workforce.[17] Entrepreneurial programs and small-business incubators are springing up on many campuses and are becoming popular with students. Another trend is to rethink how our higher education organizations work. Educational institutions are going through a period of transformation because of the increase in distance education, realignment of new programs with social and economic needs, and the growth of interdisciplinary programs. Competency-based education, loosely defined as self-paced learning tied to career development, is also growing. This model of learning is student centered and personalized to specific career goals and breaks down departmental silos. These trends promise to completely reshape the way higher education works in the future.

Other trends beginning to affect higher education, according to the 2016 *Horizon Report*, include a growing focus on measurement of learning, increased blended learning design, redesign of learning spaces, and adoption of deeper learning approaches.[18] With the rise of competency-based education and increased emphasis on education for careers, there comes a greater need to assess student mastery of learning objectives. Analytics and visualization software increasingly are being used to show student progress and mastery of subject matter. This software is now being integrated into learning management systems (LMS) to give even more detailed assessment of learning. Students indicate they appreciate timely assessment and continuous feedback such as that given in an LMS.[19] Built-in assessment is only one of the advantages of using an LMS. Increasingly, blended learning or using an online LMS to augment a traditional face-to-face course are being used to add flexibility and interactivity to learning. Students can access assignments online at their convenience, and the classroom can be "flipped" by providing readings, discussions, and tutorials online, freeing up classroom time for discussion and hands-on learning. Studies report that blended learning has been shown to increase student exam scores by engaging students in activities and providing enriched content as well as collaborative study.

In order to support these new educational methods of teaching and learning, institutions are investing in remodeled educational spaces. New space designs promote active, collaborative learning and experimentation. Since blended learning requires individual and group study areas outside of the classroom, libraries are often identified as spaces to create dynamic new study spaces in support of these new learning initiatives. These spaces also have increased technology built in for connecting to online resources, enabling online communications, and for media production.[20] In addition to these dynamic trends, there is also a growing emphasis on enabling deeper learning by providing students with opportunities to problem solve, think critically, and become self-directed in their learning. These are all goals of library information literacy instruction as well, and teacher librarians have the opportunity to partner with faculty in developing courses and resources that address these important learning objectives.

Organizations such as the American Library Association (ALA) and Association of College and Research Libraries (ACRL) also produce environmental scans that are helpful in planning future services and programs. The ACRL does an environmental scan each year that gives an overview of the current environment and outlines key trends facing libraries and the implications of these trends in planning for the future. The ACRL 2015 environmental scan discusses several trends that are changing the ways we teach and learn in libraries today, including remodeling library spaces for new pedagogical approaches, providing digital scholarship centers, creating makerspaces, the library becoming a partner in publishing.[21] Besides studying large-scale environmental scans such as the ACRL 2015 report, libraries also need to do an environmental scan of their particular environment, including the social, technological, and economic factors that may influence the future of library services for teaching and learning at their particular institution.

In looking to the future, the focus should not be on the future of the library itself but on the changes going on in the communities we serve. A curiosity and openness is needed about new directions and new partnerships in order to stay relevant today and in the future.[22] Preparing for the future is critical to libraries in order to stay relevant during changing times. It's hard to imagine all the possible futures that we can prepare for, but activities like strategic planning and scenario planning can help us to anticipate different possible outcomes and help prepare for the future. Thinking too narrowly or trying to keep things as they always have been will limit the advantages of strategic planning. In an article on the librarian as futurist, the author recommends coming up with an array of possible futures, not just worst-case or best-case scenarios but everything in between as well.[23] We can monitor trends such as those forecast in the *Horizon Report* but also follow local trends in the communities and institutions that we serve in order to prepare for future needs. At the same time, we can look at the world around us and see larger patterns and trends in society that might eventually bring about change. Higher education especially is faced with many changes, and academic libraries are taking up the challenge as they change and adapt to provide new services and teaching models. If we keep a curious and open mind and observe the local communities and global world around us, we can adapt to changes in technology, social environments, publishing models, and the ways people teach and learn in the libraries of the future.

Scenario planning, done by a variety of library and higher education organizations, has identified some recurring themes to guide libraries in their future planning for educational services. The authors of the 2013 book *Reflecting on the Future of Academic and Public Libraries* recommend scenario planning for a maximum of 15 years. The scenarios should be linked to local circumstances and used for strategic planning as well as the management of change.[24] Scenarios are a starting place for discussion and planning that will help libraries find new partnerships and collaborations, train staff, and envision new services in order to prepare for the future. One major theme identified by scenario planning is the rise of online learning, which includes lifelong learning, distance learning, and competency-based education models. A second important theme is providing education for a skilled workforce, which includes partnering with employers and developing courses that are in demand and lead to real jobs. Yet another reported theme is the partnering of colleges and universities with local governments to provide for community and regional needs in teaching and research. The focus of teaching and research can also be affected by economic forces that cause a response to state needs for public institutions or from the effects of priorities set by grant-funding organizations.[25] Some challenges that need to be confronted include decreasing staff and budgets, aging library buildings, and lack of funding for remodeling, as well as the rise of the Internet and a shift away from libraries as the primary source of scholarly information. Not all trends will affect every institution in the same way, and the key to planning will be evaluating the unique environment of each library and identifying the top opportunities and threats for each individual library setting.

In 2010, the Association of Research Libraries (ARL) created what they call the 2030 scenarios. These are a collection of several possible future scenarios for libraries. One set of scenarios cannot contain all the future possibilities across a wide range of opportunities and challenges, so multiple scenarios are envisioned. The final ARL report presents four different scenarios across a spectrum from constrained to unconstrained and aggregated to diffused changes. Ten future uncertainties or trends are identified that make up the scenarios, including:

- the nature of research,
- the nature of technological surprises,
- researchers,
- digitization and beyond,
- the research community,

- government regulation and intellectual property,
- the dynamics of knowledge sharing,
- globalization,
- economic outlook and funding, and
- the state of higher education.

The four scenarios are meant to be taken together in order to get the full picture of possible outcomes when planning for the future. The scenarios include Research Entrepreneurs, Reuse and Recycle, Disciplines in Charge, and Global Followers. [26]

The first scenario, which explores the rise of research entrepreneurs, discusses the possibility of researchers leaving the academic life in order to pursue independent research for commercial enterprises. If this becomes a growing trend, it would signal a big change for academic research institutions and their libraries as research becomes privatized. The second scenario explores what might happen if there was an ongoing economic shortage and research focus changed from innovation to reusing and recycling existing research. Research and higher education would become more focused on practical applications and job training in this scenario, and the world of tenure-track faculty would become a thing of the past. The third scenario explores a future world where individual academic disciplines develop their own technological infrastructure for data analysis and computation and split off into separate enterprises. Higher educational institutions might then become limited to a few or even just one disciplinary specialty and control all access to research in that field. The final scenario explores what might happen if academic research becomes more global and migrates away from North America to the Middle East and Asia. In this scenario, research collaboration becomes a global enterprise and remote communications technology becomes very important to those living in North America. [27]

The ARL conducted workshops with library directors using the 2030 scenarios and came up with the following common themes to consider when doing strategic planning for the future:

- Developing new relationships and collaborations to diversify revenue and funding
- Changing library values and mission as some resources and services become unsustainable
- Librarians becoming embedded members of research teams, wherever or whatever those teams look like in the future
- Research libraries won't be able to do everything for everybody so will need to focus and specialize
- Increasing collaboration between libraries and consortiums

The ARL 2030 scenarios publication includes resources for conducting workshops and planning activities using the scenarios in order to develop a strategic plan, engage the organization in planning, and keep the strategic conversation going.[28] The ARL scenarios focus on working within the research enterprise of the future, but similar scenarios could be developed for other types of libraries using the same process as outlined in the ARL publication. The goal of scenario planning is to think outside the box and come up with new ideas and solutions as well as providing a creative way to engage staff and stakeholders in the strategic planning process.

## PROVIDING USER-CENTERED SERVICES

One theme that reoccurs throughout the literature on the future of libraries is the idea of personalized services. This also corresponds with the constructivist pedagogy, which advocates for a learner-centered approach. In a 2012 book on personalizing library services, the authors promote the "boutique" approach to keeping library services and resources visible and relevant to prospective users.[29] This approach advocates for a way to transform libraries by maximizing resources, usage of services, and outreach to users by knowing your customers and providing services they want and need as well as providing excellent customer service. The model uses the case of the boutique hotel, which provides customer-centered services that are unique and highly personalized rather than generic and one-size-fits-all. Some hallmarks of this approach for libraries might include customizing every teaching session to the unique needs of the class, focusing marketing on targeted messages for specific audiences, finding multiple ways to connect one-to-one with users, and mapping out the student calendar in order to provide appropriate point-of-need learning opportunities.[30] This method puts the customer first, focusing on their needs at the time and place they need it. It means creating specific solutions for specific needs, such as providing targeted websites and information toolkits for specific groups or individual types of users. In order to do this successfully, we need to actively listen to our users and respond to their needs. This may involve increased assessment activities as well as evaluating the impact of our services. We also need to provide excellent customer service by helping users even when they are asking for something not related to our primary reason for meeting with them. Training for all library staff should be provided so that they are knowledgeable, courteous, and approachable. Complaints should be dealt with in a timely manner, and appropriate actions should be taken.

Implementing a user-centered approach may seem more daunting than providing generic services and resources typical to our type of library, but the payoffs will come through highly personalized face-to-face interactions with students, faculty, and community members who will become champions of the library and pass on their high recommendation of our services to others.[31] Communication is key to making our library services more visible. Situating librarians outside of the library in the areas where our students gather together or within the library at the point of need rather than expecting users to come to us for service and instruction is essential. While there is a trend toward online tutorials and integration into the course management system for undergraduate students, make sure these interfaces are customized and clearly branded as library services. For other, highly individualized instructional needs such as graduate student, faculty, and researcher consultations, the one-on-one approach is preferable in order to provide personalized services.

The more of these types of consultations we can provide, the more opportunities for showing the wide range of services the library can provide, many of which are unknown to those who use the library infrequently or not at all. Creating opportunities to market our services and resources is extremely important. Focus groups and surveys can provide opportunities to inform others of what the library can offer. Volunteering to serve on campus teaching and learning committees or other faculty groups can provide opportunities for outreach. Volunteering to work on student projects and activities can also provide a way for us not only to talk to students about what we do but to listen to students' needs and concerns. Our communication vehicles such as library newsletters and social media posts should also reflect a personal service approach. Content should be targeted to particular audiences, and posts should be written in an engaging and active voice and be jargon free.[32] Involving students in providing engaging and targeted social media posts can be a very successful strategy.

## FUTURE DIRECTIONS IN TEACHING AND LEARNING IN LIBRARIES

### Teaching and Learning in Libraries

As library resources become ever more virtual, libraries become less about providing resources in spaces and more about librarians teaching information literacy, both online and embedded within the communities they serve. Librarian teachers will need to increasingly specialize their knowledge and focus teaching resources to a specific audience. Librarian teachers will also need to bring their knowledge and services to where the people they serve are studying and working. They will need to regularly participate in continuing education in order to keep up with new developments in our fast-paced information and technology-focused world. Librarians will need to become community leaders and able marketers of their services in order to reach increasingly independent learners who are unaware that they are not accessing the best resources or are unable to identify the best resources for a specific information need. Librarians will need to be flexible and adaptable as well as adept at assessing services and changing models to fit new directions that arise as our parent institutions and communities change.

## Teaching Skills for Career Success

Competency-based education is emerging as a new form of higher education focused on career education and personalized learning. Hallmarks of this new model include an emphasis on student achievement of specified learning outcomes, creation of measurable learning objectives focused on knowledge and skills to be obtained, a controlled sequence of learning experiences that build on each other, and built-in assessment that measures student progress as well as mastery of specific skills.[33] Competency-based education can be applied to traditional higher education programs to offer career-aligned education that integrates traditional subject knowledge with work skills such as writing and public speaking. Critical-thinking skills and information literacy are core concepts for this kind of education, and librarians should be included with faculty as cocreators of competency-based educational programs. Real-world experiences and interactive learning are also emphasized. Interactive library learning spaces such as the active learning classroom will be in demand for this kind of teaching and learning.

## Teaching beyond the Classroom Walls

As web-conferencing software and hardware continues to improve, physical location will matter less in education. For example, we currently use Adobe Connect, Skype, and other programs to connect to webinars and teach remote sessions since our library supports a five-state regional medical school program. Our medical school recently adopted new web-conferencing software called Zoom (https://zoom.us/) that provides improved video, even over low-bandwidth connections. It has a user-friendly interface that allows multiple users to connect to the conference in separate windowpanes, and each pane is highlighted as the conference attendee is speaking. Zoom can also be used with the Kubi telepresence robot (www.revolverobotics.com/), which is an interactive stand that holds a tablet or phone and provides a Bluetooth connection so that the stand can be controlled remotely. In this way, someone from a remote location can appear on the screen of the tablet or phone and hear and speak as if they are in the meeting room where the Kubi is located. The device can be moved up or down and right and left to be able to scan the room so that the remote user can control their view almost as if they were physically present (see figure 8.2). The Kubi promises to enable more-interactive distance learning in the future.

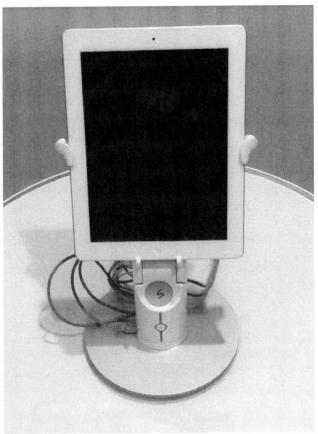

**Figure 8.2.   Kubi telepresence robot with iPad**

## Activating Learning with Multimedia

Acknowledging that all people need access to creative learning opportunities, Libraries Without Borders, the UN Refugee Agency, and other investors have created the Ideas Box, a portable multimedia kit for refugee and vulnerable populations. The box contains "tools to read, write, create and communicate."[34] Each box contains a customized library and media center with Internet access and even its own power source to be set up in the community. Different modules can be ordered, and the whole thing breaks down into boxes that can be loaded onto two pallets for shipping to remote locations. The Ideas Box is meant to supplement any existing school programs and enables digital learning as well as literacy training and self-paced education programs for adults. Some of the contents include tablet computers, laptops, a TV and projector, games, books, and e-readers as well as software, scanners, cameras, and makerspace materials and equipment (www.ideas-box.org). The Ideas Box provides education and entertainment for communities that may not have library spaces due to disaster, war, or impoverished conditions.

## Mobilizing Teaching and Learning in Libraries

Teaching and learning is becoming more mobile as students demand access through their mobile devices. Websites that are not mobile optimized are becoming a thing of the past, and many libraries are now developing their own mobile apps. The next big trend that is emerging is wearable technology. Devices like the Apple Watch and Fitbit are becoming commonplace. Teachers are also finding innovative uses for wearable technology in the classroom. Several librarians have experimented with Google Glass and explored possible library uses. Some of the newer devices have even more potential. Google Expeditions combines an app, controlled by the teacher from a tablet, that sends 360-degree panoramas to Cardboard virtual reality viewing devices, allowing students to experience virtual field trips. Some other devices with possible educational uses include the Narrative Clip and Muse. The Narrative Clip is a tiny wearable camera that allows recording photos that document a person's daily activities. The Muse headband senses brainwaves and can alert a teacher to a student's distracted thoughts or reactions to classroom activities.[35] The technology is still in development and there are concerns about privacy with some of the recording and location-aware devices, but the educational possibilities are exciting.

## Teaching and Learning in Library Spaces

At Georgia State University, an entire floor of the library was remodeled to house the Collaborative University Research and Visualization Environment (CURVE), which features a 24-foot-wide interactive video wall for dynamic data visualization. The wall is composed of multiple touch screens connected to hardware controllers and using collaborative visualization software. The space is set up with powerful workstations and collaborative furniture to allow research groups to work together on visualization projects. Some applications for usage of the CURVE space include running simulations, performing analytics, creating dynamic data visualization, using GIS software, and doing digital scholarship in a variety of fields. Students as well as faculty and research groups use the new library space, and interdisciplinary projects are fostered due to its centralized location within the library.[36]

## Learning through Creating in Library Spaces

Library space design is moving from traditional book warehouses to dynamic spaces for teaching and learning. A highly successful example can be found in the five London libraries that were reenvisioned as "Idea Stores" based on extensive consultations with people in the communities being served (www.ideastore.co.uk/). Older libraries were closed and new ones opened in the areas where people lived, worked, and shopped. Changing the name from "library" to "Idea Store" changed the negative connotation that "library" had in some residents' minds. The Idea Stores offer library resources but also online courses and extensive activities and events for the community.[37] The Idea Stores model has turned some of the lowest-performing libraries in London into the most highly rated facilities. The model's success is based on strong library and community partnerships to provide services that people need as well as providing modern spaces, technology, and making people feel at home. The Idea Stores are relevant to people's lives because they are designed and maintained through listening to community members' needs, wants, and ideas and then responding to those needs.

## THE FUTURE OF LIBRARIES IN A LEARNING SOCIETY

There will always be a need to capture human knowledge and save it for future generations, and so there will always be a need for libraries. There will always be a need to communicate knowledge in some form or another. Whether print books or e-books or some other format, there will be a need for knowledge to be curated and organized so that it is discoverable. There will be a continuing need for information professionals to help sift through the piles of human expression to find specific information to advance research and scholarship. Spaces to learn individually and in social groups will also be needed in the future. These things are needed in a society that values learning. Librarians from all types of libraries can have an effect on the future of our learning society. Equity and access to information for all are strengths that librarians bring to the table in our communities and institutions. The future of teaching and learning in libraries depends on our developing collaborations and partnerships within learning communities. Increasingly, learning in the future will be a lifelong endeavor as people strive to keep up with the fast pace of change and ever-expanding information and technology. Libraries of all kinds have a stake in the continued education of an educated society that can participate in the global economy and bring innovative and creative solutions to light for the betterment of mankind. As learning in the future becomes more mobile and web based, the type of library will matter less. Nevertheless, library spaces will still be needed to provide important pedagogical environments for deep thinking, reflection, and self-assessment.

Librarians embedded in learning environments, whether virtual or physical workplaces, labs, or health-care facilities, will also become essential to teaching and learning in the future. To prepare for this future, librarians must let go of past expectations and speak out publicly to advocate for their place in the learning society.[38] Inspired leadership is needed to bring us to the table and bring us together to make this future a reality.

Some writers have predicted the demise of the library, especially with the rise of the "Google generation." David Nicholas with CIBER Research has written that the libraries of the future will need to be seriously downsized because young people will get all their information from their mobile phones. He believes that libraries have become irrelevant and are no longer a trusted source of information. Users are turning to Google and online databases such as PubMed Central as well as social media for fast and always available Internet information sources. He recommends that librarians "go with the flow" and turn to developing services for authors such as providing bibliometrics and open access and institutional repositories. He states that librarians should "work with publishers and not against them."[39] While these services are worthy ones, I believe that traditional services for teaching and learning are not becoming irrelevant in the Google age. In this book, we have seen many examples of ways that libraries can provide more student-centered and innovative teaching, serving the unique needs of their communities. I believe libraries' ability to reinvent themselves will serve them well and bring them into the next century to continue being at the center of their communities and full partners in teaching and learning at our educational institutions.

Loriene Roy, president of ALA from 2007 to 2008, writes an inspiring essay about the future of libraries in the book *Library 2020: Today's Leading Visionaries Describe Tomorrow's Library*. Dr. Roy's essay builds on the work of Dr. Gregory Cajete, who writes about indigenous American views of teaching and learning and advocates building holistic models of education that can lead to a more fulfilling life.[40] Dr. Cajete writes about a cycle of actions that promote learning and include the following states:

- Being
- Asking
- Seeking
- Making
- Having
- Sharing
- Celebrating

In Dr. Roy's vision of the library of the future, the library promotes each of these seven states.[41] The library can be a safe place for people to be, to learn, and to develop their personal self, and the library also promotes health and wellness. The library provides an open place for asking individual or group questions. The library building can also provide a comfortable and inviting place to promote the seeking of knowledge. Libraries can provide spaces for making, where users create knowledge and ideas as well as physical objects. The library will have the resources the community needs and wants. The library will promote sharing through exhibits, events, and performances. The library is the center of the community, where people gather together to celebrate throughout their life, from youth to old age. This library of the future is thriving, and librarians are highly valued partners in new ways of teaching and learning that are needed in a society that values lifelong learning and learned, self-fulfilled citizens.

## NOTES

1. Kelly E. Miller, "Imagine! On the Future of Teaching and Learning and the Academic Research Library," *Portal: Libraries and the Academy* 14, no. 3 (2014): 329–51.

2. Ibid.

3. David Nicholas, "The Google Generation, the Mobile Phone and the 'Library' of the Future: Implications for Society, Governments and Libraries," *International Conference on Libraries, Information & Society 2014*, November 4, 2014, accessed March 30, 2016, http://myrepositori.pnm.gov.my/handle/123456789/3119.

4. Tony Horava, "OpEd—the Implications of 'Good Enough' and the Future of Libraries," *Against the Grain* 21, no. 3 (2009): 50–51.

5. Ibid.

6. Ibid.

7. Stephanie E. Mikitish and Marie L. Radford, "Initial Impressions: Investigating How Future Faculty Value Academic Libraries," in *Imagine, Innovate, Inspire: The Proceedings of the ACRL 2013 Conference*, ed. Dawn M. Mueller, 10–13 (Chicago: ACRL, 2013).

8. Gurjeet Kaur, "The Future and Changing Roles of Academic Libraries in the Digital Age," *Indian Journal of Information Sources and Services* 5, no. 1 (2015): 29–33.

9. Ibid.

10. Gail K. Dickinson, Sue C. Kimmel, and Carol A. Doll, "Common Core and Common Good: Educational Standards and the Future of Libraries," *Library Quarterly* 85, no. 3 (2015): 225–43.

11. Center for an Urban Future, "Library Funding Is Behind the Times," Center for an Urban Future website, April 2015, accessed March 30, 2016, https://nycfuture.org/data/info/library-funding-is-behind-the-times.

12. Ibid.

13. Jim Dwyer, "Denying New York Libraries the Fuel They Need," *New York Times*, April 23, 2015, accessed March 30, 2016, www.nytimes.com/2015/04/24/nyregion/denying-new-york-libraries-the-fuel-they-need.html?_r=0.

14. Ibid.

15. New York Public Library, "Historic Investment by New York City Allows Public Libraries to Offer Citywide Six-Day Service," press release, NYPL.org, June 26, 2015, accessed March 30, 2016, www.nypl.org/press/press-release/june-26-2015/historic-investment-new-york-city-allows-public-libraries-offer.

16. Peter Hernon and Joseph R. Matthews, eds., *Reflecting on the Future of Academic and Public Libraries* (Chicago: American Library Association, 2013).

17. L. Johnson, S. Adams Becker, M. Cummins, V. Estrada, A. Freeman, and C. Hall. *NMC Horizon Report: 2016 Higher Education Edition* (Austin, TX: New Media Consortium), accessed March 30, 2016, http://cdn.nmc.org/media/2016-nmc-horizon-report-he-EN.pdf.

18. Ibid.

19. Ibid.

20. Ibid.

21. ACRL Research Planning and Review Committee, *Environmental Scan 2015* (Chicago: Association of College and Research Libraries, 2015), accessed March 30, 2016, www.ala.org/acrl/sites/ala.org.acrl/files/content/publications/whitepapers/EnvironmentalScan15.pdf.

22. Brian Mathews, "Librarian as Futurist: Changing the Way Libraries Think about the Future," *Portal: Libraries and the Academy* 14, no. 3 (2014): 453–62.

23. Ibid.

24. Hernon and Matthews, *Reflecting on the Future*.

25. Ibid.

26. Association of Research Libraries and Stratus, Inc., *The ARL 2030 Scenarios: A User's Guide for Research Libraries* (Washington, DC: Association of Research Libraries, 2010), accessed March 30, 2016, www.arl.org/storage/documents/publications/arl-2030-scenarios-users-guide.pdf.

27. Ibid.

28. Ibid.

29. Andy Priestner and Elizabeth Tilley, eds., *Personalising Library Services in Higher Education: The Boutique Approach* (Farnham, UK, and Burlington, VT: Ashgate, 2012).

30. Ibid.

31. Ibid.

32. Ibid.

33. Steven Mintz, "Competency-Based Education 2.0," *Inside Higher Ed*, February 22, 2015, accessed April 5, 2016, www.insidehighered.com/blogs/higher-ed-beta/competency-based-education-20.

34. Libraries Without Borders, "The Ideas Box, a Portable Multi-media Kit for Refugee and Vulnerable Populations," Libraries Without Borders website, accessed April 5, 2016, www.librarieswithoutborders.org/index.php/news-and-events/lwb-news/item/291-the-ideas-box-a-portable-multi-media-kit-for-emergency-humanitarian-situations.

35. David Nield, "Wearable Technology in the Classroom: What's Available and What Does It Do?" *Guardian*, July 28, 2015, accessed April 5, 2016, www.theguardian.com/teacher-network/2015/jul/28/wearable-technology-classroom-virtual-reality.

36. Meg Lloyd, "Exploring High-End Visualization for Research and Education," Campus-Technology.com, July 22, 2015, accessed April 5, 2016, https://campustechnology.com/articles/2015/07/22/exploring-high-end-visualization-for-research-and-education.aspx.

37. Maija Berndtson, "'What and Why Libraries?' Looking at What Libraries Might Look Like and Why We Still Need Them Now and into the Future," *Library Hi Tech News* 29, no. 4 (2012): 13–15.

38. Dickinson, Kimmel, and Doll, "Common Core and Common Good."

39. Nicholas, "The Google Generation," 8.

40. Gregory Cajete, *Look to the Mountain: An Ecology of Indigenous Education* (Durango, CO: Kivaki Press, 1994).

41. Loriene Roy, "Loriene Roy," in *Library 2020: Today's Leading Visionaries Describe Tomorrow's Library*, ed. Joseph Janes (Lanham, MD: Scarecrow Press, 2013), 121–25.

# Index

# About the Author

Ann Whitney Gleason serves as the associate director at the University of Washington Health Sciences Library. Previously, she was the head of the Health Sciences Library at Stony Brook University in New York. Before becoming a librarian, she worked for many years as a technology specialist in higher education and K–12 education. She is also the author of *Mobile Technologies for Every Library*.